HUMANS

First published in October, 2021 by KDP.

A CIP Catalogue record for this book is available from the British Library.

Main typeset in Josephine Slab.
Printed and bound internationally by KDP and its affiliates.

FIRST EDITION

ARTWORK

The front book cover's yellow/gold paper sheep image was created by the Japanese international master origami artist Satoshi Kamiya whose designs fold inspiration from mythology, nature and mechanics. Among many noteworthy creations, his Zero fighter plane, dragon, motorbike and Cerberus are superb examples of imagination and psychology tamed by paper.

The front cover's square origami sheep, folded from mulberry paper by Gilad Aharoni, was designed by Korean origamist Jeong Ki-Dam whose work has a charming simplicity telling a good story in half the time other paper artists do, which is arguably what origami is all about.

The back cover's orange paper howling wolf creation was designed by Korean origamist Won-pyo Lee who has a very unique, strong and uniform style flowing throughout his cheerful and uplifting forms, bringing paper to life.

All of the illustrations/artwork inside this book were created by the English author Andrew Voller whose art is often inspired by trees and good deeds.

Thanks to my best friend and dad
for understanding me.

I'm a proud conspiracy realist which nowadays means I'm almost always right.

Evolution will ask humans to throw smartphones away.

ANDREW VOLLER

The Human Mind Series

Volume 1

Humans

in a Nutshell

The railroad sweep.

THE

NAKED

SHEEP

Contents

Humankind

Nature

Happiness

Society

Hope

The illustrations were inspired
by ancient tribes and the
animal kingdom.

Humankind

He's not a thinker.

Human beings in a nutshell

Let's not beat around the bush, humans are a murderous species who conquered the food chain by killing all competition standing in our way. And if it tasted okay that didn't last long either, particularly birds like the 12 foot tall Moa (extinct from 1440-45 AD), the poor dodos from Mauritius (extinct around 1690), passenger pigeons once in their billions (gone by 1914) and the delicious heath hen got roasted to extinction too (last seen in 1932). Our intrinsic behaviour hasn't changed much over thousands of warlike years. If we love or hate something, we usually hunt it down to extinction. Just accept that roughly 9 out of 10 humans are as thick as pig shit then life will be fine and dandy.

> Foxes are more intelligent than humans because they know to stay away from humans.

Man really knows how to flog fun and love to near death. Humans are a magical disappointment always sticking their meddling noses where they don't belong. We chainsaw ancient rainforests, pollute vast oceans and even poison the air we breathe. If aliens have visited our planet they probably couldn't take the futility of an insane collective consciousness perpetually moving forward without any real vision or prophecy. Lemmings don't jump off cliffs but people do. Trying to escape the pain and mental fatigue of living in such a mad society is what turns us into airy dreamers and moody fantasists. Most oddly, happiness and enlightenment are way down our list of priorities. Humanity is a marvel to behold, full of accelerated inventiveness, an obsession with turning ourselves into robots or clones and of course producing nuclear power just in case we ever feel the need to blow ourselves to smithereens. The fact we haven't already annihilated the planet with radiation is highly commendable. People are a mass of positive potential wasted because of our cowardly inability to stand up to greedy bullies hellbent on global despotic rule. The frightening thing about globalism is there's no point running away from tyranny to another country. We have wiped out most of the world's wildlife so it makes sense we'd turn on ourselves next. Humans have failed. Perhaps it's time we listened to our pets instead.

There is a lack of love in the world and you can make a difference by sharing your warm heart with people cold from loneliness.

But the pitiful human saga has not remotely been all bad either. What other animals have crowds in stitches of laughter watching their comedy show. The list of positive human achievements is nothing short of phenomenal. Humans invented the wheel, music, language and writing, boats, art, farming, bread and wine, the Gutenberg printing press (moveable type), bicycles, electricity, computers, aeroplanes, Penicillin, sewers and indoor plumbing, refrigeration and even cheeseburgers. One of the most mind-boggling inventions ever is the Constantinesco synchronization gear which perfectly timed machine-gun fire through millisecond gaps in the spinning blades of a plane's propeller. And humans have also explored the world with fantastic style and panache in balloons and biplanes, yet mostly with courageous grit and determination on foot and through rough seas.

Humans are capable of being far greater than we are right now.

For some people, just showing up for life is a great achievement, yet some humans have done miles better than that. From roughly 1300-900 BC the Lapita culture, most likely originating from Taiwan, were some of the Polynesian ancestors who used outstanding wayfinding navigational techniques to sail across thousands of miles of Pacific Ocean to find the Hawaiian, Society and Samoan Islands and many more onto Easter Island and New Zealand. The Maori settlers of New Zealand were devoted to harmonizing with nature, creating gods for the elements, sea, forests, etc. Their mythology believed the demigod Maui created the Hawaiian Islands by anchoring his famous fish hook (*Manaiakalani*) to the sea bed and then tricked his brothers into believing he needed help to land a huge fish by getting them to paddle as hard as they could to raise the islands one by one. Legend also has it that culture hero Maui lassoed Kala (the sun) with a rope made from his sister Hina's hair, demanding the days were made longer in summer so the people could catch more fish and grow more food. Yes, humans come up with untold levels of nice nonsense to spur us on and to fit convenient social narratives.

Roughly two thousand years later, around 10th century CE (Common Era), the great Norse explorer Leif Erikson from Iceland, son of Eric the Red, was the first known European to discover North America which he named Vinland (Land of Wine). He was known as Leif the Lucky because of his courage, adventurous spirit and making his own luck. Leif's historic longboat voyage from Greenland with a 35 man crew inspired numerous Viking attempts to colonise the New World. Despite some peaceful trading, the indigenous peoples (ancestors of one group called the Innu, meaning 'human being') naturally did not take kindly to the Nordic foreigners pillaging, raping, killing and enslaving some tribal members who they called *Skraelings*. Consequently, many skirmishes over a number of centuries eventually contributed towards the end of the Norsemen's North American seafaring.

From then to now, the immoral profits of human trafficking have always been the catalyst for foreigners turning up on shores and ruining poor people's lives. In 1492, Cristoforco Columbo of Genoa took his first of four voyages from Spain to the Americas and immediately set about enslaving and violently mistreating the indigenous Americans who also had no immunity to Eurasian diseases like smallpox. Columbus' much lauded sailing discoveries became the native American's worst living nightmare.

During its late 16th century peak, galley slaves at war could barely stay alive on minimal sleep and a meek diet of a watery bean stew, or gruel and vinegar water, biscuits dipped in wine, or stale bread. Most died of disease from cuts and whip wounds, starvation and exhaustion, and were then unchained and unceremoniously dumped overboard to the sharks. Surviving that inconceivable level of torture with very little hope of seeing out a 10 year maximum sentence could possibly be the greatest human achievement ever.

There is clearly no limit to how much greedy humans exploit members of their own species if they can get away with it which is why we must always fight oppression before cruelty roots into our psyche as a warped, accepted norm. Peace is an island surrounded by oceans of violent history and slavery. Similarly, multiculturalism is a polite term for simultaneously upsetting the balance of multiple communities on purpose for economic gain and has never worked because people rarely change their beliefs. The lovely idea is that everyone gets along nicely, increasing their knowledge and wisdom by learning about other cultures. But in reality most people don't mix and just stick to their own kind whilst feeling resentful their standard and way of living has diminished. First-rate intelligence is seeing the ship of truth sailing through a rough ocean of seaweed lies.

Moving forward about 340 years to 1911, the Norwegian explorer Roald Amundsen and his company of 4 others successfully became the first ever humans to reach the inhospitable South Pole. Their valiant achievement was famously overshadowed by British explorer Robert Falcon

Scott and his team also making it to the Geographic South Pole just 34 days after Amundsen, where tragically all 5 men died on the return journey just 11 miles away from depot safety. We can only imagine the psychological devastation on discovering the Norwegian flag had beaten the Brits to the pole, followed by the desperate hopelessness weeks later of running out of rations and also fuel to melt ice and frozen food.

Scott's ill fated expedition even saw over a dozen killer whales circling a group of their ponies on an ice floe panicked into falling into the freezing water and only one managed to swim to safety. Conclusively, Amundsen's superior decision to use sled dogs to pull his team's equipment made the critical difference over Scott's mixed transport of motor-sledges, dogs and ponies. However, for various unfolding reasons the original plan to have Scott's team resupplied by a dog team 300 miles from Hut Point failed miserably, leaving the last three frostbitten explorers without hope. Rather than being angry with being let down so terribly, in his journal Scott magnanimously wrote,

"No-one is to blame and I hope no attempt will be made to suggest that we had lacked support."

Unable to continue and not wishing to slow the remaining team down, Scott's companion Captain Titus Oates bravely decided to walk to his death alone, recorded as saying,

"I am just going outside and may be some time."

Despite making major errors in preparation with perhaps a smidgen of hubris clouding his judgement, Scott and his team's stiff upper lip approach and stalwart character symbolizes the high principles and pride humanity is capable of. They had strength and humility and that's the very best you can ask from any person.

Don't ask too much of people because most of them think soap operas are documentaries.

Humans are opportunistic risk takers who've accelerated through evolution at breakneck speed. Early modern humans have been a fairly short walk in the park compared to other species roaming the Earth like insects and reptiles, yet we learnt how to control fire, found and forged bronze, iron and steel, and made enough amazing machines to wreck lots of the planet in some way or another. Humans have even fished the gargantuan oceans to epic levels of scarcity. However, millions of kind people do their best to save animals and treat their pets with love and respect. It's almost exclusively the pond life at the top who have no regard for living things. If you think the people in charge of society care about you, you're quite simply bonkers. Unwavering compassion for your fellow humans is the nexus to a successful society.

It's really frustrating seeing how truly great humanity could be if everyone cared more about morality than money.

Fifty eight years after the two renowned South Pole expeditions, and without a shadow of a doubt humanity's greatest achievement, humans landed on the moon. To be able to gaze upon planet Earth from our proper natural satellite in the solar system seemed unbelievable at the time and that's because it never happened. Moon landings are one of many very big porky pies our leaders have told us for glory, dominion and mainly money. The weird people in charge script their own social narrative regardless of the truth. We live in a topsy-turvy world where the truth is condemned as misinformation, but heinous lies are given the thumbs-up and green light. Science and a plethora of hard evidence prove that humans never set foot on the moon or even got close.

For a start, all of the moon landing film footage and photos can easily be discredited as fake and the moon movie featuring Neil Armstrong and Edwin 'Buzz' Aldrin was almost certainly shot by legendary director Stanley Kubrick, filmed in Area 51 in the Nevada high desert. Notable photographic anomalies include the American flag waving in zero atmosphere; there's no blast crater under the lunar module; one of the moon rocks made out of papier-mâché has a large prop letter C clearly written on it; the sun shadows come from studio lights at different angles to the sun; there are identical backgrounds when the astronauts were supposedly at different locations; and quite mysteriously you also don't see any stars in space. And of course the light-sensitive photographic film itself would have disintegrated when exposed to high radiation. To top that off, a number of NASA astronauts accidentally or purposely admitted in interviews that no man has ever set foot on the moon due to inadequate technology. One astronaut called Don Pettit amusingly said,

"I'd go to the moon in a nanosecond. The problem is we don't have the technology to do that anymore. We used to but we destroyed that technology and it's a painful process to build it back again."

That's right, NASA kept every last lying fragment of moon landing stage props and fake rocks for museums, but they accidently destroyed arguably the most important technology in America's history as well as all the telemetry tapes too. They didn't even have the brains to say it was destroyed in a fire, opting for it was just somehow lost. Top comedy and a transparent hoax. I conclude 5 main reasons why humans never landed on the moon:

1. If they'd gone to the moon, NASA wouldn't need to fake film footage and photos of Earth using low grade technology to disguise their trickery. A common sign of any individual or global lie is the lack of real and decisive information available often mixed in with airy-fairy facts. When researching global lies, all official articles tend to avoid solid evidence in favour of waffle. And if they do show rare detailed facts, they immediately and intuitively strike you as having many anomalies which don't add up.

2. It's very odd that no country ever went back to the moon. The superpowers would do anything to build a space station on the moon and launch craft from there taking space exploration further than ever. China's Chang'e-4 mission claims are very easy to discredit: the film makers even left embarrassingly large chalk lines on the studio floor which was supposed to be the moon's surface.

3. The Administrator of NASA, James Webb, resigned just a few days before the launch and all three Apollo 11 astronauts also resigned soon after their staged return to Earth. Neil Armstrong never gave an interview again after the post flight press debriefing. These are not the actions of deserved heroes who would have loved to lap up the limelight and cash in, but rather the decisions of professional, frustrated men disgusted at being made to lie to the American public.

4. Despite every last nook and cranny of space and ounce of weight being critical to successfully making it to the moon, the following Apollo missions 15, 16 and 17 somehow each managed to take a moon buggy weighing over 200 kilograms on Earth, at 7.5ft long and 10ft high.

5. It's not possible for humans to survive the Van Allen radiation belts which are two giant doughnut shaped zones of energetic charged particles captured by Earth's magnetosphere. Less than 1/8th of an inch of aluminium certainly isn't going to stop you getting fried by dangerous particles in the outer belt reaching up to several hundred million electron volts. This is the most compelling reason why manned deep space travel is game over for now. There are many scientific calculations and models explaining how astronauts can safely travel through the Van Allen Belts without suffering from fatal levels of ARS (acute radiation syndrome), but on closer examination none of them have mathematical credence or practical application. The hard fact remains that every manned space mission in history from 1961 to now (Vostok, Mercury, Gemini, Soyuz, Apollo, Space Shuttle, Shenzhou, Spaceship 1 & 2, Dragon 2, Salyut, Skylab, Mir, the International Space Station and Tiangong) have all been well below these deadly rings of radiation for logical reasons. In 1958, a Geiger counter on Explorer 1 satellite registered Van Allen Belt radiation levels at roughly 1000 times higher than in normal space. If space programs could go higher they would love to, but obviously they can't. End of investigation. To solve this huge seemingly insurmountable invisible barrier, the Americans detonated a 1.4 megaton nuclear bomb named Starfish Prime at 250 miles above Earth in 1962 which simply added even much more radiation. If in doubt, blow it up should be humanity's motto.

There is a wicked conspiracy going around that world leaders have our best interests at heart.

Humans find it terribly difficult to separate myth from reality because they generally fear new experiences which aren't planned. Safely flying a man to the moon and back is only a bit more likely than it being made out of cheese.

NASA claim the Apollo and Lunokhod landers left 5 small retroreflectors (mirrors) on the moon which they can reflect powerful laser pulses off, proving without question they landed there. If we naively take their word for it, because that's all we have, this doesn't categorically *prove* anything. For a start, not only could the laser beams be directed off the Lunar Reconnaissance Orbiter (if that really is orbiting the moon), but robotic spacecraft may have made it to the moon and set mirrors in place. More realistically, many astronomers say it's perfectly possible to moon bounce radio waves and laser beams off the lunar surface itself without any deflecting device which cancels out all suspect talk of retroreflector proof that people walked on the moon. It's a thousand times easier to swallow a government lie than to find out the real truth all by yourself.

If everyone told the truth, eventually there would be nothing to get upset about.

Next they'll be telling us stars are lost glow-in-the-dark golf balls floating in space and people will believe. It should be difficult to trust global companies that receive trillions of dollars of taxpayer's money when only they have the technology and responsibly to prove their own work is valid. The generally held mistaken notion it's totally unbelievable that tens of thousands of people can somehow all be involved in a mass secret lie or government conspiracy is defunct and doesn't understand how embarrassingly obsequious and obedient most humans are. Most humans are lackey copycats surrounding a minority of good eggs who stand out with integrity.

People really don't like any change to their lives unless it's a holiday, especially if they're on a gravy train, so thousands of lecturers, astronomers and computer technicians involved in the space race will happily keep a sizeable fabrication going to protect their cushy job. In the same vein, thousands of employees such as salespersons, advertisers, graphic designers, doctors and lawyers working for the cigarette industry knew for decades how damaging smoking is to millions of people's lungs, yet kept silent to remain employed. The thalidomide scandal, asbestos cover-up and the 2020 American general election vote counting fraud are just a few more good examples out of hundreds where thousands of everyday people swept the truth under the carpet because that's the easiest option and it benefitted them. The bottom line is boat-rockers get fired and finding a new job can be stressful and difficult so people row over the truth and sometimes help drown it if no-one is looking.

> All science nowadays goes to
> the highest bidder.

Using highly effective false advertisement campaigns, all the authorities have to do is convince the people it's for the greater good - even though it almost never is - and most people won't mutiny. It's almost frightening how your long held opinions change if you take the time and trouble to look down a few scary rabbit holes. Financial dominance keeps people in check and in debt. Money is king, queen, emperor and unquestioned ruler of the universe we know and operate in. Practically all thoughts of anarchy are easily whipped into control by threatening non-compliance with abject poverty and imprisonment..

It turns out over 6 million years of hominid evolution got it wrong because the year 2020 said people's immune systems don't work after all.

Only a genuine person with principles, a madman or fool would jeopardize their job and family's future by shooting themselves in the foot in the revered name of honour and truth. When it's in a persons best selfish interest to contribute towards a global financial deceit or fraud by looking in the other direction, absolutely nothing stops millions of people benefitting from their own quiet conformity and co-operation rather than biting the hand that feeds them. For instance, well over 10 million doctors worldwide have known for many decades that vaccines are largely ineffectual, yet can damage your immune system and cause death. They are perfectly willing to keep promoting those jabs which kill thousands of people worldwide on the false pretext it's for the good of herd immunity.

Hundreds of other harmful medicines were and are handed out by doctors like candy in a sweet-shop regardless of their known dangers, such as sleeping pills, opioids, the pill and statins. If drug dealers who deliberately hand over substances they know harm people are classed as criminals, then most doctors are also criminals. Doctor's don't sign the Hippocratic Oath anymore and it shows.

> A world without doctors might
> actually be safer and healthier.

Disconcertingly the well-known pharmaceutical company J&J (Johnson & Johnson) who paid damages of over 2 billion US dollars for selling products they knew caused ovarian cancer, have also developed a covid vaccine known to cause blood clots, causing numerous fatalities. In two legal cases in 2010 and 2011, courts forced J&J to pay $166 million in total for misbranding drugs and hiring doctors for their sales team to push medical products for unapproved, off-label purposes. In 2009, pharma giant Pfizer pleaded guilty to illegally marketing an arthritis drug and agreed to pay a record $2.3 billion healthcare fraud settlement. It seems there is an endless bandwagon of corrupt doctors prepared to harm people for financial gain – par for the course – yet most people still trust doctors even though in America, doctor error is arguably the 3rd biggest killer (2016 study), let alone the promotion of misdiagnosed prescriptions. Just like astronauts, doctors like to think of themselves as high and mighty heroes but back down on planet Earth doctors are just unprincipled and glorified peddlers of poison and their mistakes are one of the biggest causes of death.

> There are probably a lot more
> doctor serial killers than we realize.

For over 50 years the cures for most cancers, like cannabis oil and eating or avoiding certain key foods, have been deliberately suppressed to support the billion dollar chemotherapy and radiotherapy industry which statistically kills more people than it cures. They create cancer with some prescription drugs, pesticides and foods soaked in buckets of sugar and then cash in on the chemo'. This cycle of greed is how everything in our society works, often making problems from nothing. Many effective natural remedies developed over centuries with no side-effects have been poo-pooed because they don't make corporations money. Money controls people's integrity levels. In most countries, doctors readily prescribe toxic medications and treatments to billions of people without a care in the world on the behest of big pharma because earning in excess of 5 times the average wage buys their silence and unquestioned loyalty. You can be happy in a deceitful world as long as you don't become the lie.

A miniscule percentage of courageous and good souls will put their livelihood or neck on the line to defend the truth and when they do they're either sacked and ridiculed or even lose their lives in mysterious circumstances. Therefore, far from it being impossible that massive lies would not surface if huge amounts of people in an organisation are involved, on the contrary, the larger the amount of accomplices, the more accepting people are at covering up and working with the lie as an accepted norm. Plus, how are you going to find out about any controversial leaks and damning information exposing the truth when there's no free press anymore. We rarely get to hear the courageous voices of disgruntled whistleblowers because they are frozen out of all media coverage.

When you tell people the truth about global psy-ops and government corruption they act like you've turned to the dark side just for describing it.

Humans are currently living in one of the most extraordinary and phenomenal periods in history where an entire species have been tamed and subjugated by two electronic devices known as smartphones and the goggle-box. Buying into bullshit fashion trends and stupid memes, etc, is the resultant mindset of a materialistic mainframe which knows how to control its citizens with bread and circus technology. One of the easiest and best things you can do to unmask global agendas, experiments in worldwide mind control and challenge false narratives, is delete your Facebook account. More than anything in the whole world, we need a global news channel reporting uncensored truth.

Everyone in the distant past knew that the poor, unfortunate souls sentenced to burn at the stake for supposed devil worshipping had possibly upset someone of higher social rank before confessions were tortured out of them or were just unlucky, random pawns. No doubt, in most cases the victims had done virtually nothing wrong, but everyone goes along with the heinous deceit because standing up to a corrupt church was fatal. In fact, it's very important that tyranny maintains oppression by sentencing totally innocent people so everyone else stays petrified it could be them next if they step out of line. Modern human beings mostly live in fear of not protecting group consensus and walk around all day long defending little white lies, half-truths, shameful skeletons and even wicked, gross injustices. To suggest huge lies for profit and dominion can't be put into practice, controlled and silenced, especially on a global scale, is simply naive and untrue. Billionaires take turns at being the Wizard of Oz. The same dimwits who believe the central banking system is organic, that free markets exist and oil prices aren't controlled also believe global scams by united governments are impossible. Seeing through government lies is essential to mentally escaping this financial paradigm and psychological regime.

> Death is inevitable. It would just be nice if
> our leaders didn't help speed up
> the dying process.

There's no logical reason whatsoever to believe that big business haven't bought up entire countries and infiltrated and controlled their politics to promote sinister agendas. Thinking otherwise is downright wide-eyed and simple, and shows less understanding of world affairs than horses have. Simultaneously bribing whole countries, their top leaders and civil servants to promote false reasons to sell global pharmaceutical products or the desperate need for space, defence or nuclear programs, is much easier than most people would imagine because *their* organisations also own the banks printing the money they lend to those countries. Corporate monopolies, via the governments they bankroll, create fake emergencies as lucrative business plans all the time, such as global warming. Ocean water levels have remained roughly the same for centuries, yet numerous gigantic counter measures for a problem which simply doesn't exist have been promoted to the heavens, making lords of crime trillions of dollars whilst far from helping, damaging the environment instead.

Where do people think electric car power comes from, the air?

One of many good examples is the global wind turbine scandal where more energy and pollution is caused by producing, transporting and discarding the huge chucks of steel towers and monopiles, the concrete foundations, the nacelles and generators and the non-recyclable fibreglass turbine blades (longer than a Beoing 747 wing), than energy is gained and saved. Graveyards of thousands of these immense structures slowly leak pollution into your water table, all in the name of pseudo-science, pretend sustainability and certain corruption. Despite reams of manipulated data and statistics available, in real life a wind turbine is like a greedy bee that eats more honey than it produces. Not to mention the tens of thousands of birds they kill every year too. The same energy saving disinformation can be said about tons of recycled products. Maybe by the next ice age the climate change doom squad will finally admit global warming was a monumental business plan, not a reality, hence why halfway through their bogus campaign they had to change the Global Warming slogan to Climate Change because they couldn't prove global warming existed. Average people seem to have a total and utter, Hobbit-like inability to comprehend how corrupt united nations are all working together to return us to default poverty and slavery. Only when they lose their jobs, homes and savings will they wake from the villainous hypnotism they've fallen under. You can't defend your children if you don't know who the enemy is.

Tyranny takes over when millions of people aren't prepared to lose their jobs to defend principles.

To conclude our space exploration and fraud investigation, the whole man on moon escapade is a series of combined impossibilities on an average massive journey of 477,710 miles to the moon and back again. The odds against no technical or human problems sabotaging the mission are so high you'd have a higher probability finding a television executive who isn't dungeon deep in paedophilia. Astronauts would experience uncompromising conditions in deep space where moon surface temperatures range from an average of 125°C to minus 203°C surrounded by lunar dust which cuts like glass whilst soaking up about 60 microsieverts of radiation per hour, which is about 200 times more than on Earth. Taking back off from the moon in the Eagle LEM (Lunar Excursion Module) to successfully reconnect with CM (Command Module) Columbia alone was fraught with countless opportunities to fail. Plus, how have we apparently gone over 50 years backwards in technological advancement too? And who was holding the camera beyond robotic arm reach when Neil Armstrong took his first step onto the moon or when the top half of the lunar module disconnected from its base and took off from the moon? Perhaps it was a friendly alien happy to help the new space tourists and send the film through intergalactic post later. Way too much of most people's core knowledge comes from made-up rubbish on the television.

> You can lead sheeple to books but
> you can't make them read.

The Apollo missions weren't a giant leap for mankind, rather a gigantic lie wasting millions of dollars which should have been used to save millions of starving people on Earth instead. What actually happened in 1969 was the Saturn V rocket successfully took off and jettisoned its engines and the three astronauts hung around in Lower Earth Orbit for a day or so as the Earth TV space show aired. Then they re-entered our atmosphere without being crushed or burnt to a cinder, which is a noteworthy achievement because the re-entry corridor is only a few degrees narrow and the spacecraft also had to withstand temperatures as high as 3000° Fahrenheit (1,650°C) whilst not rotating out of control at speeds of nearly 25,000 mph. The crux of the con is what the FAI (International Astronomical Federation) define as outer space, the Kármán line (62 miles high), isn't really space. Beyond the dreaded Van Allen Belts is the real outer space.

On the face of it, it's all well and good trying to explore the universe, yet humanity can't even successfully explore or tame its own mind and motivations. All the trillions wasted exploring space would've been better spent building an underwater city we could actually visit. We believe we're a brilliant, curious nomadic animal who can eventually understand and conquer anything, but technology has turned many of us into keyboard warriors and couch potatoes. Our reality needs to be burst wide open if we are to survive.

If the people in charge would lie so blatantly about something as big as moon landings or general election results, then what else are these absolutist sharks capable of lying about and more importantly WHY are they lying? Perhaps pretending to search the unfathomable universe is not only about lining their pockets with coin but a beguiling way of scaring us? Follow the money and you find the evil. It's frightening how much they tell us about life isn't true and even more worrying is how most people prefer the lies. Not only does the shocking moon hoax make you not trust governments, but it gets you to question what shape the universe and planets are. Perhaps stars are tiny holes to the real world outside.

It turns out that most of what you learned at school was propaganda lies.

Once you work out for yourself the only moon walk humans ever did came from Michael Jackson, or delve into layers of conspiracy from other big lies like the Star Wars defence program or the Piltdown Man paleoanthropological fraud, you can start to unravel the monstrous web of deceit and misinformation that shrouds most historical records in your century. The minority of very wealthy humans are usually barefaced liars who ruin reality by rewriting history to suit their coercive agenda, whereas generally speaking, the happy-go-lucky masses just make do. The really evil stuff comes from the top and upsets our morality and perception of authenticity.

Most people also have a negative tendency to see the whole world as bad when things are going bad for them personally. Human beings struggle a lot with perspective and handling unstable emotions. The predominantly violent beast within finds it hard to reconcile with layers of restricting etiquette and social dogma. Our very confused and conflicting species has yet to find metaphysical balance, thus the majority of us muddle along doing our best for family and friends on a daily basis. The overwhelming majority of people are pretty decent souls full of kindness and altruism, especially when given the time and energy to excel. We are all subconsciously connected to one another as orbs of energy rotating on a river blue and lush green planet. The universe created your energy for good reason so don't throw your life into a black hole when the stars don't shine on you.

Kindness, forgiveness, humour, empathy and love are the five pillars of human progress, all housed under the main roof of compassion. Without the ability to empathize with a stranger's misfortune, humanity would never have formed strong enough emotional bonds to create small protective tribes. A world without empathy would be aggressive, mercenary and suicidal, overtaking parental instincts. Sympathy is a stepping stone to empathy and empathy another healthy stride towards an enlightened state of mind. We all have a natural ability to empathize; how much so depends on where your conscience lies on a spectrum of good and evil. Evil never ceases until you mentally and physically stop it.

Therefore, I conclude humanity's greatest achievement of all-time is something the majority of people do very well: bringing up their children with love and kindness. Historians often measure great endeavours as physically challenging, landmark events we could probably never do ourselves, like circumnavigating around the world or swimming across the English Channel. However, building a well balanced family is one of the most difficult things in the world to accomplish.

A Sunday afternoon roast cooked by a mother that loves you is the pinnacle of life.

Humans rear their offspring longer than any other mammal which is the foundation of all other great achievements (second place goes to orangutans who may nurse their young up to 8 years old). It's one level to climb Mount Everest, yet an even higher summit of success producing a happy child who goes on to enrich the lives of others as an emotionally stable adult because meeting a sane person nowadays who doesn't want anything from you is rare.

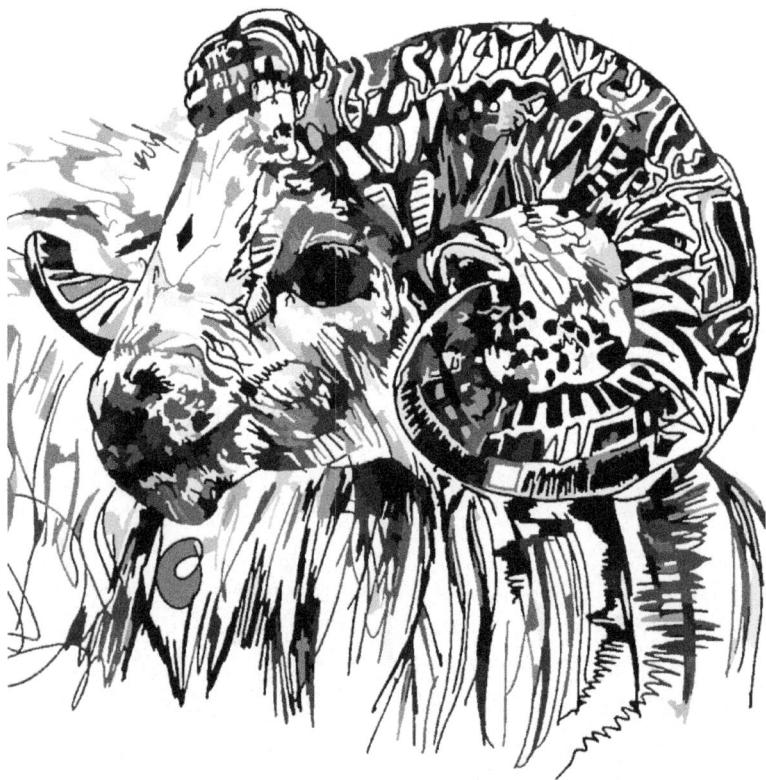

A sheep with balls.

Sheep factor maximum

Belief is more important to people than reality. Somewhere along the line, truth became almost illegal. When feeling just mild psychological pressure, most people couldn't care less about science or rational thought and subconsciously want everyone else to be as unhappy and scared as they are. Their blinkered compliance resents a free thinker's normality and independence because they're losing control so crave one-dimensional thoughts. In a state of prolonged anxiety, if government medical advisors said putting a golf ball up people's butts prevents catching yet another made-up virus, golf balls and petroleum jelly would sell out in a day. That's how stupid humans are. Putting your head in the sand by doing whatever your corrupt government tells you because you're scared is not a smart or helpful way of behaving. People will believe anything you say if you repeat it enough, then give them a gold star to confirm they listened well.

> A huge amount of people don't
> question or read anything.

Humans are designed to mimic behaviour which unfortunately makes most of us embarrassingly gullible and shamelessly impressionable. We learn and feel comfortable repeating and perfecting actions over-and-over again until they're second knowledge. The skilful qualities which made us excellent carpenters or blacksmiths, etc, also mean we are easily crafted, forged hot and cold, and manipulated by psychological suggestion because we like to follow set patterns until our taxed minds reach a place of familiarity. There's a psychological comfort in routines which no amount of spontaneity can compete with. But the more people obey nonsensical routines, the more they will do as they are told by higher-ups until the frightening echo of slavery takes our homes and freedoms away again.

Sheeple possess no curiosity to find out the truth, they live in fear and have little pride. Consequently they're oblivious to reality and easy prey for corrupt authorities.

Throughout history there are countless examples of the rich and powerful lying to the people in order to keep control and power. Often a natural disaster or genuine pandemic like the Black Death was used as the catalyst to introduce a campaign of fear to suppress the development of free minds and beliefs. In the European witch trails (roughly 100,000 cases) somewhere between 10,000 60,000 innocent people were executed, of which approximately three-quarters were women. The first horrific organised witch-hunts began in 1428 in the Canton of Valais, Switzerland where the peasants previously staged a determined insurgency between 1415-20 against the oppression of the dictatorial Raron family. Instilling the fear of death into the poor people to prevent further rebellion, Valais authorities came up with the cunning plan of causing division in the populace and turning people against their kin and community by encouraging false accusations of witchcraft, sorcery, murder and being in pact with the devil, probably mostly directed at unpopular neighbours. By branding random innocent individuals with crimes against God, the citizens lost focus and unification fighting the powers that be, until only desperate thoughts of survival against inexplicable, vicious madness were ingrained in their minds. To be arrested and imprisoned as a heretic you only needed public talk or slander by 3 or 4 neighbours and if 5-10 in number you'd be tortured. Doing this ensured a scared sheeple mentality had power over courageous minds.

Among many bizarre accusations with no supportive evidence whatsoever, some victims were accused of flying through the air, being werewolves and making invisibility potions. If they really could summon those powers then they could escape being arrested. Extreme, unimaginable pain inflicted had a way of getting people to reliably confess to any crime they never committed. Then their innocent souls were either tortured to death, beheaded or most commonly tied to a ladder with a bag of gunpowder hung around their neck and tipped into the fire – going out with a bang, from where the idiom possibly originated. By getting the people to reinforce heinous government lies, their grip on reality and willpower was greatly diminished.

Fear is our greatest Achilles' heel. Once there to help us it now keeps us pinned down if you can't transcend the matrix.

This almost unbelievable mass hysteria spread throughout Europe from about 1450-1750, reaching an hysterical peak between 1560-1630. In 1563, the Dutch physician Johann Weyer wrote a bestseller called On the Tricks of Demons where he tried hard with a medical scepticism to make people see how senseless the witchcraft persecutions were, arguing that the accused were suffering from mental illness, not witchcraft - psychological delusions rather than deliberate attempts to conjure supernatural forces. Instead of being burnt at the stake for opposing the authorities system of oppression, Weyer's works remarkably helped the Netherlands put an end to the madness of witchcraft trials. Perhaps Dr Simone Gold's contemporary bestseller I Do Not Consent will become as influential with regards to the coronavirus pandemic in years to come.

> No need to psychoanalyse the sheep because they're not deep. Sheeple simply believe everything they see on television without question, full stop.

If the sheep get sheared anymore they'll be serving themselves mint sauce. Many centuries of fear-mongering has shaped humans into the sheep-like creatures we are today - the intense fear of torture possibly part of our genetic memories. The masses have been whipped into obedience so many times because mentally crushed people chose suicide over assassination of the demons causing their pitiful plight. Humankind keeps allowing tyrannical cults to systematically subjugate the working classes, herd people like sheep, tag them with laws, mark us with labels, judge, then sentence everyone who is born and dies with nothing. Over many centuries of coercion, imposition and scheming social conventions, people have been conditioned to accept devious government policies as the norm. The most important aspect of destroying people's human spirit is to make punishments unjustified, random and completely unfair to simulate death's randomness by reminding the plebs that anyone at any time can become a victim, therefore making everyone subconsciously fearful and never fully settled – giving you a powerless feeling that nothing will change no matter what you do, which simply isn't true. The people are less afraid of slavery than dictators are of revolution.

Every century humanity needs to have a good spring-clean of corruption and proper decluttering of evil people.

Thousands of years ago, either the idea of God was invented or God's word was hijacked by evil forces with the soul intention of controlling the masses. The net result of a few millennia of manipulated minds is sheepdom. Especially since World War II, people have been led down the garden path into a false sense of security, becoming mentally soft and weak. Contemporary humans are the most delusional they've ever been because we've got more time on our hands than ever to explore our imaginations and dreams, and up until recently most countries have not been subjected to dictatorship rollouts and archaic modes of subjugation. We don't want a return to the kind of fear where every thought and move you make is double-checked dare you offend your power-crazed master.

The sheer amount of people lying to themselves on what life is about is phenomenal. Most people have become willing foot soldiers - more like fodder - of globalist cult buying frenzies with their knee-jerk, fad behaviour. They will regularly buy good for nothing cancer culturing sugar packed products from Starbucks and McDonalds not only because of convenience, but mainly a bad, set in their ways habit of mistrusting small companies without brand name and television status. People bow down to repetition and feel safer with impersonal, barcode scanned experiences and this disenfranchisement erodes whole communities.

Work your whole life to receive a paltry pension before they put you down. That's an even bigger con than pyramid schemes.

Scratch beneath the surface of globalist eco-friendly bullshit and you'll notice literally hundreds of possible examples of global corporate logos symbolising demonic and occult ownership, and Illuminati worldwide dominance. For example, the Gmail envelope looks like a modern re-working of the Masonic Royal Rich Apron and Facebook's F is fairly similar to the Masonic Tubal Cain. Apple's famous bitten apple logo may represent the forbidden fruit and exile from Eden, and perhaps the serpent in the World Health

Organisation logo is from the Garden of Eden too, not from the Rod of Asclepius or Baphomet (the WHO logo also has 33 segments and 33 can represent the number of fallen angels. That world symbol, like the UN emblem, is also surrounded by laurel leaves which are a common symbol of victory, but were also used to fashion wreaths in ancient Rome). Much hidden occult and esoteric symbolism shrouds modern society and veils evil agendas. It's actually surprising how truly childish the Illuminati can be, thinking they're being really clever disguising hidden meanings, duplicitous imagery and subliminal messages in everything we see when most people are so brain-dead it doesn't even enter their subconscious.

Many conspiracy theorists think the Australian $20 dollar bill released in 2017 has got a magnified virus design with the covid spike proteins on it as clear as daylight, which don't look like Australia's flowers of the golden wattle plant emblem as official sources suggest. Certainly the new polymer British £20 note also has a similar looking spiky virus on a purple foil patch on artist Joseph Turner's side, coincidentally issued on 20/02/2020 when the Covid-19 pandemic started to take off in England. However, the twenty pound note design could easily be from Tate Britain's staircase where Turner's magnificent work is often displayed and this whole paragraph clouded with conspiracy.

Sometimes conspiracy theorists need to curb their enthusiasm. Not every famous person is a trans imposter with silicone ears. Once you set off on a road to uncover the truth – if you haven't already done so – you'll encounter lots of genuinely mad and bizarre theories based on zero physics or logic, where the inventor of fantasy has become so addicted to exposing government and world order lies they often overlook basic scientific facts and eternal values. It's natural to develop antipathy towards public organisations and institutions who are supposed to protect us but in reality fuck the people over a barrel. Yet hatred has a nasty habit of making you believe all evidence against your enemy, be it made up mumbo-jumbo or crystal clear facts.

Nevertheless, if most conformist type people knew how much the rulers of the world are laughing at their sheep-like ignorance they'd be shocked, upset, depressed or downright angry and might actually do something about it to return the balance of power to the people. Instead, most shuffle along like robots on a factory conveyor belt and mob anyone who questions the government's and media's take on things. You have to spoon feed the sheep information one choo-choo train at a time otherwise they'll spit the truth out.

Humanity is so delusional it needs weekly therapy sessions with the Bible's wisdom.

Governments are just price tags for global corporation products. Defending people who mug you daily is the epitome of gullibility. Yes, in real life there are a few handfuls of James Bond like super-powerful villains with trillions of dollars – so wealthy they aren't even talked about much – twiddling their thumbs while stroking a cat wearing smug, cold-blooded grins as they work out how to reset humanity back to the bleak condition of feudalism and Roman slavery, meanwhile loads of us stuff our faces with burgers thinking the eighties freedom is going to last forever. Being a conspiracy theorist often comes with the unenviable, heavy burden of being a smart ass who's right nearly all the time but sounding like you're wrong or just plain mental.

Some rude awakenings will definitely shock billions of people in this next decade as they are forced to learn about Agenda 21, the spurious HIV pandemic, the Secret Owl Society, BlackRock and The Vanguard Group buying up houses and literally everything, Event 201, Pizzagate, Antoine Béchamp's terrain theory, the Georgia Guidestones and adrenochrome harvesting. Once you begin or continue your journey of truth, you'll never want to look back or bother with closed minds again. When fake friends sacrifice your freedom to alleviate their fear, make it a pithy goodbye in favour of *rabbit hole* reality. Don't let the truth overwhelm you though, rather enjoy every step of the way as light shining through a crowded social canopy. In the meantime, most of the proletariat remain blinkered and blissfully unaware that society is not remotely organic as God or the universe intends it to be: everything you are allowed to do is controlled and plastered with adverts. Through fear of change or refusal to accept the truth, people are caught up defending old lifestyles and freedoms that have already rapidly been erased, deleted and replaced by frightening Orwellian laws which mean you can be arrested and detained for literally anything, having done absolutely nothing wrong.

To fit in nowadays you're expected to queue up for your own death certificate.

In 2020, humanity already embraced witch trial type hysteria where refuseniks who don't follow irrational mob consensus were reported to the police by their neighbours. But just like 400 plus years before, the people going along with and supporting the madness for petty jealousies, rivalries and daft non-scientific reasons are the real mad ones, not those refusing to be a party to a campaign of government lies to save their skin. Obviously the authorities want to cull brave people because they're the only ones with the heart to fight tyranny. If you're living in fear about anything you've got life all wrong.

Imagine being so devoid of spirituality you actually believe your government.

One thing the sheep are brilliant at doing is depressing everyone around them. Sheeple get very upset hearing the truth but have no problem repeating a huge lie which hurts you. When we patronisingly describe people as sheep, what we generally mean is subservient, mindless, fearful, spineless and back-stabbing people who don't think twice about grassing up their neighbours, friends and even own family members for petty social infringements. With the exception of Karens, I do not mean that sheeple are people working in a controlled office environments or similar because a job is a job and nearly all of us are pinned down by financial pressures sometimes compromising our opinions, beliefs and integrity. A high or low sheeple factor is all gauged on your levels of personal courage, thirst for the truth and willingness to step back from the crowd and think about what you really feel on a subconscious and spiritual level. The day you selfishly stop caring what's right and true is when you turn from one of the real people to sheeple.

> A conspiracy theorist is basically anyone who can be bothered to do some proper research.

Investigating conspiracy theories that turn out to be true will fire your mind up. The sheep commonly call anyone who has original and truthful ideas a Conspiracy Theorist but at least you haven't got gullible branded on your forehead. After years of watching the sheeple huddle together in frightened flocks, critical thinkers develop contempt for them because the drones drag us all down with their blind compliance and cowardly levels of irrational fear. The sheer mass of deeply stupid people who want to be afraid of anything is the only thing we should be afraid of. Everyone who believes New World Order lies has yet to overcome their fear of dying. Paradoxically, facing up to the world's troubles is best way for all of us to escape them. The sheep complying with tyranny become accessories to their own suffering. We need to stop worrying what's coming around the corner and start doing something about it before it's too late.

If you're right, most people won't agree with you but will find it much harder to admit the truth than see it. We rarely question anything until suffering trauma or tragedy. Humans are really good at pointing out other people's mistakes whilst completely ignoring their own. Sheeple always make the mistake of assuming that worrying is the same as thinking.

The amount of free, critical thinkers who can objectively assess any situation or problem without succumbing to any peer pressure or government conditioning is much higher than most people assume: I estimate about one fifth of the population and Solomon Asch's conformity experiments concluded one quarter of people consistently went against majority opinion (under no threats of intimidation or violence). Yet, only a tiny fraction of those independent minds are financially secure, characterful and confident enough to face the consequences of saying the truth out loud. Plus, disagreeing with everyone zaps energy and means you really have to know what you're talking about.

The year 2020 transformed crazy conspiracy theorists into divine oracles.

It's so maddening that people who discover and speak the truth get turned into outcasts for being right. The phenomenal dynamic of social conformity is immense and far outweighs our inventiveness and life dreams. This obsequious state of affairs is one of the few factors from our ancestral nature which isn't helpful and badly holds us back. Obviously in the wild, being ostracised meant almost certain death, therefore we are programmed to put up with a lot of abuse before turning away from the tribe. Isolation to a teamwork animal equals perpetual fear and panic. Yet in a our jam-packed, listless society your own voice should be the first voice you listen to and being ostracized is frequently a good thing. Being alone is often your best option to guarantee good company. One clear advantage of our lonely and vacuous communities is you can choose to not give a fuck about what virtually anyone thinks without being lynched or outcast. Having a pet is often the best lifestyle choice. Less than 1% of cats or dogs might let you down, whereas over 99% of people are likely to let you down. Conclusion: get a cat and/or a dog. You never thought you'd like people on social media a lot more than acquaintances, friends and most family in real life, but here we are.

Don't drain yourself educating the sheep.
Half of them will never get it
even in the afterlife.

Do you ever feel like you're being played? Wear a mask, take the knee, stand 6 feet apart, stay in your home, don't go for a meal, talk less, don't make eye contact with other people, don't fart because it spreads viruses and the list of restrictions will go on forever as long as the sheep keep swallowing lies until we learn to take charge ourselves. We have to feel really sorry for teenagers these days. Their lives should be starting to take off making new friends and dating instead of being shutdown by insane tyrants who want their blood and energy. Millions of people aren't coping very well in these demented times because of hateful mega-wealthy mad men deleting your freedoms as fast as Pac-Man, so it's your civic duty to stay on top of your emotions and not be mentally beaten by evil. The globalists have divided communities up like counting coins in their banks and now plan on making it a cashless society which gives full control of your life over to centralised banking. They want us all unemployed and living on benefits so we have no control over our lives and then must obey harmful and austere rules just to eat. These unelected world rulers have created a society shitty enough so that most of us don't want to know each other.

Have you noticed how the greater good only benefits wealthy people.

A society that so easily turns its back on truth is at breaking point, ready to erupt like a volcano. Once you find out no planes hit the Twin Towers and bombs dropped them you have to accept the West was hijacked by satanic powers with rotten carcass minds many decades ago and it was only a matter of time before they tried to enslave you.

Enjoy as much quiet and silence of the mind as you can because an evil storm is coming.

Kill shot. (Painted in 2009)

Cognitive dissonance is rife

The moon landing hoaxes were a huge immoral waste of money, yet admittedly elaborately magnificent and almost romantic, still fooling most people today. The Counter-Reformation witch trial inquisitions were a very clever plan to spread panic and fear throughout villages and towns, shaking the foundation of community stability and human courage. However, both of those grandiose lies to the general public pale in significance compared to the Covid-19 global conspiracy.

Global warming is as fake as the covid virus.

Most humans appear to be totally delusional by nature and the perfect showcase for this psychological fact is the 2020, never-ending covid pandemic which is the most fascinating example *ever* of how easy it is to brainwash your average person. We react best to visual stimulus, so all the heartless leaders in charge had to do is blitzkrieg people's minds by showing them a few dead bodies in hospitals on every TV channel in the world every minute of the day, buy loads of doctors to say there's a dangerous pandemic and this instilled the fear of God into virtually everyone. Is humanity going to survive? Answer: millions of people think Bill Gates is a hero and saviour of our planet. The sheep are never going to admit they were fooled by this pandemic are they?

In 2020, billions of people went completely batshit crazy, became possessed with fear and totally wet the bed over an unidentified, invisible virus which thousands of eminent scientists across the world have put their reputations and jobs on the line to claim that the SARS-CoV-2 virus (which causes the Covid-19 disease) has never been isolated, purified or cultured in laboratory conditions, fulfilling Koch's Postulates, which they say means there's no proof it even exists. Their professional opinions almost never get aired on MSM and thousands are dismissed as mere conspiracy theorists despite previously distinguished careers as physicians. The general public are unaware that people have proven in court cases the covid virus has never been isolated. Calling it a conspiracy theory saves sheeple the trouble of thinking for once.

So much good in the world never sees the light of day because we don't stop evil stepping out of the shadows. When you watch a video of rows of people in India lying in the street pretending to be dead for a media photoshoot with crowds around them laughing as they reposition themselves and then you see it on the news later as Covid-19 tragedy, it makes you feel like you're being played for a fool. Other staged films show mannequins and plastic bags stuffed inside rows of body bags and even old photos of genuine past tragedies, all masquerading in the media as heavy covid death toll pandemic evidence. But perhaps they're just faked videos on social media made by crazy conspiracy theorists? What really is going on? Lots and lots of other covid things don't add up:

Firstly, all pandemics follow the Bell Curve theory but covid doesn't care about science and has more variant curves than Marilyn Monroe. The next strain of covid bullshit should be called the Pinocchio variant. The world is full of real and dangerous variants including poverty, starvation and suicide. In 2021, former Chief scientific officer and Vice President of Pfizer, Dr Mike Yeadon, made it remarkably clear saying,

"...the variants most different from the Wuhan sequence was still 99.7% identical. I can assure you that there is zero - not just implausible - but zero chance of something that would escape the immunity of someone who was immune from natural infection or vaccination. It's absolutely impossible, no matter what they tell you."

Secondly, this is the only so-called pandemic in history where the death count (2020) is roughly the same as the normal years before. If you don't think that's suspicious then your cerebral cortex is not normal either. If everyone was dying left, right and centre like in a real pandemic, there would be no doubt or debate about covid's existence. How comes burial and cremation figures in the UK remained the same in 2020, in fact many funeral directors said quieter than in 2019, even during reported spikes in covid deaths? And why are perfectly healthy, asymptomatic people considered medical cases? Furthermore, how can the world's population increase by over 81 million (2020) in the middle of a pernicious pandemic?

Thirdly, flu has almost totally disappeared, which is scientifically impossible. They hijacked the flu and called it covid just like car thieves change the number plates. Winner of the 2013 Nobel Prize for Chemistry, Professor Michael Levitt calculated covid has an average survival rate of 99.95% which coincidentally is approximately the same as influenza. They swapped the flu for covid as fast as Clark Kent changes into Superman and neither are ever around at the same time. Anyone who believes covid killed flu has had their little grey matter fried by fear.

Covid-19 must be dangerous because it killed influenza, brain cells, backbone, common sense, fun and it even managed to prepare for its own arrival.

It's alarming how common colds, influenza, pneumonia and centuries old coronaviruses suddenly transformed into Covid-19 after months of doctored death certificates, banned autopsies, scaremongering, panic and hyperventilation. Such is the power of the mind you can make yourself ill just by worrying you might catch something when you're totally fine. You can convince your conscious brain any paranoia is real if you put your mind to it. The anticipation and fear is for most people much worse than the reality. Anxiety alone can make you ill or even suicidal, so try to stay calm at all times by keeping a healthy perspective. Experience shows people who do the least research about Covid-19 have the most anxiety. Also, the more schooled and wealthy a person is, the more likely they are to believe the covid scamdemic which shows that education is worthless and money deludes. If the sheep ever realise they got scammed by covid the shock will be like accidentally finding out they were adopted. Now over one and a half years in and it's mind-boggling how so many people don't understand this pandemic is fake. Cognitive dissonance sounds professional but a better diagnosis is called being thick. The sheeple are suffering from global hysteria and hypnosis. A blind man can see this pandemic is not real. This is by far the worst pandemic of medical and leadership lying humans have ever experienced. Even one poor sod in Britain who died falling off a ladder was put down as covid for his cause of death. It's a mountainous climb to change someone's mind after they've been brainwashed by scaremongering. The best way to help people overcome huge irrational fears is to present a much bigger real fear. Death only ruins one day so it doesn't make sense ruining all the other days worrying about covid. What we all really needed was a virus that could only be cured with kindness.

Bigfoot is much more likely to exist than Covid-19.

When the world's leading medical centres were asked by numerous scientific institutions to prove the novel SARS-CoV-2 exists, they declined to do so which is the scientific equivalent of the dog ate my homework. Similarly, a large number of global freedom of information requests got many government medical authorities to admit that no isolates were available. Also, in a 2020 interview, Dr Wu Zunyou, Chief Epidemiologist from the Chinese CDC said,

"No, they didn't isolate the virus. That's the issue."

In addition, the UK government, Public Health England and the Advisory Committee on Dangerous Pathogens did not classify Covid-19 as a high consequence infectious disease (HCID), downgrading it way back on the 19th of March 2020. Further delving into the truth also uncovers that a number of safe, highly effective and affordable exiting treatments for coronaviruses, such as HCQ (Hydroxychloroquine) and Ivermectin were discouraged from use or even blocked in many hospitals for unexplained reasons, almost as if the whole thing was planned for profit.

Even more concerning, how does one account for all of the countries which totally ignored the pandemic, believing it a hoax, having minimal or absolutely no lockdowns or unnecessary restrictions, yet had no increase in their overall mortality rates whilst caring on as normal: Belarus, Nicaragua, Burundi, Sweden, Tanzania, Madagascar, Turkmenistan, Brazil, Russia and many more. Even the claimed origin of Covid-19, China, who were caught-out filming many fake victims pretending to drop down dead of covid in the street, had virtually no lockdowns after the initial scaremongering and fear porn campaign and also fully recovered without using the vaccine. Not to mention Belarusian President Aleksandr Lukashenka who claimed he'd been offered $940 million USD to pretend his country had a deadly virus and to crash his country's economy. Strange that US Amish communities haven't reported being ill from covid or any other deadly virus either, nor the Inuit, Aboriginal tribes, the homeless and drug addicts, covid protestors, many travelling communities, Columbian and Albanian drug cartels and the Taliban; all groups who mix with outsiders and foreigners. We greatly underestimate the power of our psychosomatic imagination to invent reality when fear strikes us down with cowardice.

> The idea of long covid is
> a hypochondriac's wet dream.

One of the greatest voices of reason and no-nonsense speeches during this plandemic came from top pathologist Dr Roger Hodkinson (Cambridge University, Corpus Christi College, MA, MB, B, Chir. Royal College certified general pathologist (FRCPC and FCAP). Recognized by the Court of Queen's Bench as an expert in pathology and also CEO of a biotech company that actually makes covid tests – are his impressive credentials). In a Canadian conference on the 13th November 2020, Dr Roger Hodkinson dared to speak the truth, saying,

"The bottom line is simply this: there is utterly unfounded public hysteria driven by the media and politicians. It's outrageous. This is the greatest hoax ever perpetrated on an unsuspecting public… It should be thought as nothing more than a bad flu season. This is not Ebola, it's not SARS; it's politics playing medicine and that's a very dangerous game… Masks are utterly useless. There is no evidence based on their effectiveness whatsoever. Paper masks and fabric masks are simply virtue-signalling... Social distancing is also useless... Everywhere should be open tomorrow as was stated in the Great Barrington Declaration... And a word on testing... positive test results DO NOT, underlined in neon, mean a clinical infection. It's simply driving public hysteria and all testing should STOP... the risk of death under 65 in this province is 1 in 300,000... You've got to get a grip on this. The scale of the response you are undertaking, with no evidence for it, is utterly ridiculous given the consequences of acting in a way that you're proposing. All kinds of suicides, business closures, funerals, weddings, etc, etc, it's simply outrageous. It's just another bad flu and you've got to get your minds around that. Let people make their own decisions... You're being led down the garden path..."

But of course, hardly anyone ever heard his magnificent speech because mainstream media banned it. They only report government lies nowadays. They lied about weapons of mass destruction and now they've created one. The sheep just can't accept that a global fraud and depopulation scheme of this magnitude is possible to organise because they think small in a big bad world.

Sheeple want the truth if their partner is cheating on them but don't care about trivial things like global genocide. People who believe governments and big pharma have their best interests at heart show a level of gullibility which dives straight into the shallow end of mental illness. If they lied about going to the moon and the Twin Tower's explosions, then they'll have no problem lying about this pandemic either. The covid plandemic is like weather forecasts: they bombard you with satellite charts, fake historical data and complex algorithms, but to find out what it's really like all you have to do is open the curtains. If there was a super deadly coronavirus, most supermarket checkout employees would probably be dead by now.

The people who believe this pandemic is real are the same fools who give their bank details to scammers over the phone.

In a kind of wartime spirit vibe, billions of well-meaning mugs believe by wearing flimsy masks and obeying illogical rules they're helping to fight a deadly virus, clueless to the only real enemy being propaganda. It's painful watching people who consider themselves educated and intelligent standing there like ignorant fools with masks on, socially distancing because the TV told them to.

Viruses are about 1,000 times smaller than the width of a human hair and the last 40 years of global medical research before 2020 says non-surgical masks have an insignificant, negligible or non-existent impact on preventing the spread of viruses. The largest coronavirus diameter (0.14 microns) is roughly half the size of the holes in most face masks (0.3 microns). Oh, but larger water particles carrying the virus no deadlier than influenza could kill me, worry the sheep hiding under their bed covers on plastic sheets. In real life, virtually no-one coughs or sneezes directly in your face. More to the point, people habitually touch their face lots wearing masks which more than doubles your chance of infection. Wearing a non-surgical mask to stop viruses is like putting an umbrella up inside to stop the rain outside. Masks are only there to make you ill and silence your beliefs. You could climb a mountain of discarded masks and never get covid because it's a fictional virus. Light up your life by burning all masks. Our natural immune systems are 100% better at fighting viruses than any masks and synthetic vaccines. Furthermore, if you allow your child to wear a mask you are an uniformed and bad parent because numerous scientific studies show it damages their physical and mental health, as well as social development.

Bedwetting masked men who harass women without a mask in shops really are the epitome of cowardice.

Masks not only take away oxygen and can give you bacterial pneumonia if worn for too long, they also remove your identity. Wearing a mask won't stop viruses but it does put an end to smiling. And anyone with half a brain agrees lockdowns don't do anything but destroy lives. This is a media pandemic not a scientific one. It's not a real pandemic if they have to advertise it on every news channel otherwise you'd never know it was happening. The key to the greatest heist of human minds in history is the fraudulent use of a polymerase chain reaction test (PCR) deliberately run at too high a cycle threshold. Also, there's been some great stand-up shows recently but nothing beats watching people take lateral flow test results seriously. Everything about convid is a false positive and the only thing they isolated is the people.

If the Nobel Prize winner who invented the PCR test, Dr Kary Mullis, thought it shouldn't be used to test for viruses then we should probably have listened.

We understand billionaire Illuminati psychopaths think of us as lab rats, we know most politicians are barefaced liars and it's common knowledge most journalists have zero professional integrity who parrot their master's bidding, but few of us thought that millions of turncoat doctors would aid and abet this unprecedented scale of medical deception by going along with it without objections., costing millions and potentially billions of lives in the near future. More doctors have abandoned the Hippocratic Oath and care of duty in this scamdemic than rats fled The Great Fire of London.

One of the biggest mistakes you can ever make is putting your full trust in doctors because it's amazing how many shy away from scientific facts. Trusting doctors and politicians nowadays could cost you your life. The harsh and critical reality is many doctors are narcissists with a god complex who drain you for all you're worth and don't care if you die. Largely because of doctor's not going on strike in defence of their patients' well-being and human rights, the masses have fallen for the Covid-1984 con, hook, line and sinker. Have we really got to such a low point you have to be your own hospital and doctor from now on? Millions of people have been praying since day one hoping that all doctors and nurses would develop some courage to speak up about what's really happening because that might very well end this nightmare scam. Fingers crossed the mounting vaccine deaths will help the majority of medical professionals grow a conscience.

However, not everyone is the bad guy who betrays innocent people because they were 'just doing their job'. With courage and resilience in the face of overwhelming odds, a band of global doctors are calling this pandemic panic in play, a scam, a swindle and a global crime. True class can't be bought or even fully taught, it's something you're either born with or not.

> The sheep genuinely get angry if you're not losing your mind about a fake pandemic like they have.

Observing the sheep struggling with the truth is like watching a kid's toy running out of battery power. Smart people have desperately tried to warn family and friends this is not about a virus but social control, money and depopulation plans, yet the sheep don't want to see any real science data and are deaf to common sense and truth. If you take away people's reason for living, they become obsessive compulsive, hypochondriac germaphobes who sanitize their hands red raw. The high fear factor has made sheeple switch off from reality and obey without questioning like a misguided and bonded cult of fanatics suffering from Stockholm syndrome. Vaccines and masks have become their initiation process like tattoos and drugs were to ancestral tribes. It's almost like they really wanted a deadly disease to turn up, so at long last they have something valid to moan about or focus on. On the plus side, some people are much more appealing wearing masks. The sheep are embarrassingly closed-minded and will rarely admit they are wrong. If you red pill sheeple the truth, they go into psychological lockdown akin to autistic behaviour. Little can be done to help such blinkered, small minds. Leave them be in their misery and move on.

It's now dawning on millions of people that covid is a bad cold and the most profitable scam in human history.

Carrying their straw man arguments inside their pea-brains whilst shuffling down the street, possibly avoiding cracks in the pavements too, the covid fans exhibit very strange and offensive behaviours indeed. Some jump into bushes out of an innocent child's way like paranoid lunatics just in case they catch something in the open air. Others hold their breath and turn their heads walking past people and elbow bump instead of shaking hands. A few of these oddballs even shout at and follow strangers around supermarkets who don't obey government shill guidelines. They are the type of people who wear masks in their own home and put masks over car air vents or clean the post before opening it. Some hikers in the middle of nowhere are wearing masks or walking in see-through tents with not a soul around for miles. It has become common practice for many people to soak their takeaway food and drink covers with anti-bacterial spray. And it's embarrassing watching musicians playing wind instruments through slits in their masks. Perspective hasn't just gone out of the window, it's buried itself six feet under too. These once normal-ish humans have lost the plot and many transformed into virtue signalling attention seekers covering their fear with comfort blankets. Lots have been observed using a diving snorkel or wearing a fish bowl over their head.

The real covid idiots won't do any research because the truth will frighten them even more. 2020 onwards is one of the most interesting, revealing and unhappy times in human history, like a dystopian horror novel of epic proportions, especially when people take covid avoidance to ridiculous and unloving extremes like some abusive parents who in real life shut their own children in their bedrooms after school and leave food outside the door to avoid the 'virus'. And what's happening inside thousands of care homes is nothing short of mass murder. Two shocking words: Midazolam and Remdesivir. Ventilator flow valve pressures were set dangerously high as well.

If you're not allowed to question it, it's evil.

Billions of suckers are in a covid brainwashed trance like Pavlov's dogs and we'll never experience so many mentally disturbed people on this world again who turned down the red pill of reality. All of these previously straightforward people have lost their marbles, become positively unfriendly and many are nasty little snitches and paid truther harassers too. They seem to heavily resent covid deniers and vaccine refuseniks being anxiety free and happy, so they try to shame, gang-up on and get angry with non-mask wearers for not falling into their confused trap. Honestly, the sheer brass neck cheek of clueless and selfish people getting really bitter and twisted you're not afraid of a fake pandemic like they are is astounding.

Sheeple don't care about right and wrong but just want to feel like good guys so they can condemn the pretend bad guys and feel less guilty about their cowardly and ignorant ways. These huge flocks of sheeple are the true crazies who readily call other people mad for not being comfortable living a lie like they are. When huddled together in delusional masses it's surprising how nasty the sheep can be. The church of covid is a dark place where foolish worshippers chant their own downfall. The only thing the sheep are good at is sinking the human race. Every minute you spend talking to the sheep is time wasted you'll regret.

The sheeple are in a state of shock and denial. Lord there is no helping these media hypnotised people. It takes character to admit you were fooled by a hoax. When you discover you've been lied to it's human nature to defend the lie rather than admit you've been a duped. If you believe this pandemic is legit, one day you'll feel like the biggest fool on Earth. Covid-19 is the largest IQ survey conducted in the history of humanity where most people failed the i part.

Humanity is great when we help each other out. If we could just stop getting divided by lies we'd be on the road to freedom. No matter what you believe, 2020 was likely the biggest eye-opener of your life. At the end of the day there's lots of very good people who got cruelly misled into believing Covid-19 is new and real, who shall die as a result and that's enormously sad whatever side of the fence you're on. However, if you find out your dragon mother-in-law is having both covid jabs, don't hold back your happiness.

This is the only world war in history where the people are literally queuing up to be shot by the enemy.

Common ancestors to coronaviruses have been around for over 50 million years, so humans are very used to them. In fact, when physicians record a patient suffering from a cold, they used to write down coronavirus as the diagnosis. We were first led to believe that the Chinavirus was a novel/new deadly virus which may have started through the consumption of bats bought from wet markets in Wuhan, or from a leaked man-made virus in one of the test laboratories in Wuhan. Both original source claims were never proven and remain iffy.

Many well extremely respected doctors who insist this is not a real pandemic, Professor Dolores Cahill for one, assert that SARS-Cov-2 is merely SARS-Cov-1 renamed and remarketed as Covid-19, which is an already existing coronavirus named in 2003, showing similar symptoms to colds and flus, almost as if it were a cold or influenza. If the PCR covid test is run incorrectly, which it has been on an industrial scale, it can easily pick up a whole host of other illnesses including the common cold, influenza A and B, Ebola, rabies, hepatitis C and E, West Nile Fever, Polio or measles as well as the elusive Covid-19 because it cannot distinguish between *live* virus and non-infective RNA, producing a huge number of false positives.

After virologists examined over 290,000 SARS-Cov-2 proteome sequences (published, January 2021) deposited in GISAID (the Global Initiative on Sharing All Influenza Data), only 27 of the proteins with Covid-19 mutated at different rates (notably the prevalent D614G and P323L in the spike), yet out of the hundreds of thousands of proteomes with little to no mutational variability, scientists still didn't isolate the Covid-19 virus which shows it's either impossible to isolate, they didn't want to isolate it for bizarre reasons or most logically it doesn't exist. Despite multiple claims of isolation and purification which have all been easily discredited, to this very day the Covid-19 virus has *never* been categorically proven to exist. Clowns who think this pandemic is real probably believe Jeffrey Epstein is an innocent children's party organiser.

The sheep don't want to hear a single word of scientific truth because it exposes their embarrassing levels of stupidity.

The main problem with the claims of isolation, apart from the lack of independent peer reviews (if it is possible to even isolate viruses which potentially mutate millions of times) is scientists can use computer modelling to achieve favourable outcomes. In brief, using computer models is gene bank deception, creating something from nothing. Computer programme predictions can be wildly inaccurate, basically taking one small string of codes and filling in gaps where real data doesn't exist to create the whole sequence: they are notorious for providing false conclusions.

Another fraudulent angle described by the determined and methodical virologist Christine Massey MSc, explains that frequently medical institution's claims of Covid-19 isolation provide no proof of isolation (purification) without contamination from other genetic material, often monkey kidney cells and fetal bovine serum. A different type of commonly used computer modelling deception was seen in 2005 during the supposed bird flu outbreak. Using computer/mathematical modelling, a UK government funded professor - bankrolled by big pharma - predicted up to 200,000,000 bird flu deaths. In reality, in the last 20 years much less than a thousand people worldwide have died of bird flu and those figures are dubious. It's easy to manipulate cases, gene sequences, death rate predictions and scientists if you pay them enough. The fact that viruses have been patented by the organizations profiting from the vaccines to prevent independent scientists looking at the data, is very suspicious too. The proof of isolation pantomime continues. If we can't categorically prove Covid-19 exists through science or drastically increased global death figures, the only logical opinion one can reach is the whole pandemic is a hoax for profit and control.

> It's just too big a mental leap for most
> people to accept this pandemic is
> all based on a total lie.

Apparently there is a terrible pandemic ripping havoc, misery and death throughout the world. You'll notice though it's always somewhere else and never in your neighbourhood or on your doorstep: 1984 to a T. I'm no doctor or virologist and have never professed to being so, but I can read and think independently from corrupt global propaganda. I'm just an avid amateur researcher and conspiracy realist keen to find out the truth behind so many incongruities, odd coincidences, countless red flags and blatant lies. Consequently, aside from expert medical opinions presented, my conclusions are mostly based on my thoughts, some guesswork, intuition, probabilities, undoctored statistics and common sense conjectures which could simply all be wrong – although that's not been the case with other topics I've examined in similar detail.

I conclude there is no Covid-19 at all and that SARS-Cov-1 and hundreds of other commonly circulating flu and cold type viruses have been recorded and rebranded as Covid-19, all being lumped onto the covid business bandwagon and agenda with statistical anomalies everywhere you look. Reclassifying every cold and flu case in the world as covid is very misleading, like recording every panic attack as a heart attack. If you subtract other illnesses being classed as covid, then covid has the same amount of deaths as flu and flu has disappeared. You don't need to be a brain surgeon to figure out what's going on.

Billions of people are suffering from mass psychosis caused by a malicious bombardment of fake news. To the people who say a deadly virus was released or *there must be something,* how do you account for a good dozen or so countries who haven't played the covid game, having no excess deaths at all? To repeat, the impossible worldwide disappearance of influenza should be enough on its own for any rational mind to conclude this is a fake pandemic created by manipulating statistics. Coupled with roughly the same amount of global deaths in 2020 as normal pre-pandemic years and it's a no-brainer. From day one to now the wildly inaccurate covid testing process has always been the kingpin to creating a false pandemic or casedemic – where no UK Nightingale 'overflow' white elephant hospitals were needed. There is no specific violent coronavirus surging throughout the world. Statistical manipulation and bogus testing is the disease. All health organisations still haven't categorically proven the covid virus exists simply because it doesn't. Everyone should care about this a lot more. I bet there are some cats and dogs who've worked out it's a scamdemic by now.

Common tragic covid scenarios: they're elderly and scared of covid then catch a bad cold or flu. The fake test says positive so off to hospital feeling awful and panicked. They're put on a ventilator set too high and now they're fighting for they're lives. They die, it's recorded as covid and the hospital gets a big bonus. Alternatively, they're frail, in an old people's home and bullied into taking the vaccine without being allowed to see their family during lockdowns. They die of vaccine side-effects and/or other medication administered, that's put down as covid as the cause of death and the home gets their dirty money. Shameful crossed over to criminal ages ago.

If covid was real and dangerous, most teachers would be dead by now after mixing with children from hundreds of different homes.

Much evidence coming to the fore shows it was all planned years beforehand: Lock Step 2010; 2018 Clade X; the 2012 Olympics opening ceremony; the 2005 Aaron Russo interview; Operation Mockingbird; Bill Gates' depopulation Ted Talk; WHO Disease X 2018; Obama 2014 pandemic speech; governments paying farmers to destroy crops; Fauci's 2017 surprise outbreak interview; DR CREEP 2013 song called PANDEMIC; intelligence organization Deagel's 2025 population predictions; the September 2019 GPMB's A World at Risk report and cover; Instagram's AR (Augmented Reality) face masks filter trend started in 2017 to get youngsters used to wearing masks; 2018 IDM (Institute for Disease Modeling) video; the $100 billion covid contact tracing deal 6 months before the plandemic; and a potential covid vaccine developed by Moderna was sent to the University of North Carolina researchers 19 days before the emergence of Covid-19.

In addition, many countries have bought millions of body bags and stackable plastic coffins. Mega-prisons and numerous quarantine camps are being built, some with built-in crematoriums next door. Is there something we don't know and how can they predict the future? Two apocalyptic words: Marburg and ricin. They are literally telling you a series of pandemics are planned. Just 3 weeks to flatten the curve turned very rapidly into you'll own nothing and be happy about it, and some people still think this is about a virus. Lord help us. It's time for people to reboot their minds and wake up to reality. The only deadly thing going around is stupidity.

If the whole world unplugged their TV for a week or two, people might start snapping out of their covid trance.

Mix together media brainwashing, a peppering of paranoia and panic, add shovels full of fear to a nasty cold and you have created Covid-19. We don't link a belief in covid to mental illness enough. An independent mind is the greatest shield against evil intentions. Millions of people will never to their dying day admit they got hoodwinked good and proper by this plandemic but as soon as the remaining sheep do, we can try to recreate a much better old normal together.

Being in a deep state of anxiety for over a year and a half about a virus that scientists still haven't categorically proven exists is the definition of insanity. The real madness lies in sheeple doing no research themselves whatsoever about something that has profoundly upset their lives and minds. They're going to create new variants, new viruses, new vaccines, new pandemics and new nonsensical rules forever until we give them a taste of their own medicine. Hopefully we'll live long enough to enjoy the day everyone has to admit the Covid-19 virus only existed in name, not reality. That may never happen, but you must believe in the medical truth eventually coming out and those responsible for this deadly hoax will be sentenced for crimes against humanity. When loads of crisis actors, famous actors and politicians clearly faked having the covid vaccine so blatantly on television, you must question why. Also, during pandemic peaks would thousands of medical staff from around the world have the time and energy to choreograph loads of TikTok videos? More importantly, if the covid vaccine is safe and effective, why were millions of those doctors and nurses so reluctant to take the jab?

Most people who are anti-vaccines have done lots of research about vaccines.

The human species held their intelligence in the highest of esteem until this plandemic reminded us we're just dumb apes who copy behaviour without thinking. Think how disappointed millions of soldiers who risked their lives for our freedom would be if they saw people squandering basic civil liberties and human rights away because of apathy and blind stupidity. We need more men that will go down with a sinking ship rather than dress up as women to save themselves. It's true we're in a coup and war without bombs where people are accidentally helping the enemy through ignorance and fear. The peasants have nearly been conquered without a single bullet being fired. Global warfare without bullets being fired is very confusing to most people. In 2020, five leaders of the Ivory Coast, Eswatini (formerly Swaziland), Haiti, Tanzania and Burundi all allegedly opposed and banned the covid vaccines from use in their countries, and within roughly 6 months they all died. Maybe they died of covid?

> You're living in a dictatorship when you continue to lose your rights no matter how much you comply. That's where we're at now.

Above all other concerns, understand that nobody has any authority whatsoever to make you take any medicine you don't want, says The Nuremberg Code of 1947: "The voluntary consent of the human subject is absolutely essential" (Permissible Medical Experiments, point 1). It's your body, your choice and that's a hill everyone should be prepared to die on in defence of their children's future. Bullying and forcing billions of people into having any medical procedure against their will, under the false pretext of being for the greater good, is nothing short of blackmail, tyranny and democide. In fact, doing so is pure evil. The covid plandemic is the world's largest ever crime scene.

You have to seriously ask yourself why in 2020, over 1000 top lawyers from around the world, including the world renowned trial lawyer Dr Reiner Fuellmich and over 10,000 highly qualified and internationally respected medical experts would risk their lucrative careers and personal safety by taking our world leaders to court for crimes against humanity, known as Nuremberg 2. Has humanity really learnt nothing from the Holocaust?

The great reset of our lives is upon us and hopefully it will be recorded in history as the great awakening, not the great cull.

Every century, humans get caught in a rut of being trapped by evil then escaping being slaves but this is not our destiny and needs breaking from like an abuse victim saying no to a narcissistic relationship. An unbalanced economic and dog-eat-dog society is not only designed to make you unhappy but also to forget what happiness is. Humanity currently has a serious gullibility problem caused by losing the true purpose and point of living. Convincing perfectly healthy, asymptomatic people they could be ill, really was a masterstroke of manipulation.

One great thing about Covid-1984 is open-minded people have found each other in large numbers.

Governments seem to be capable of making virtually anyone do anything if it convinces them everyone else is doing it. Never before have billions of fools been successfully gaslighted by their governments in the most magnificent brainwashing enterprise in human existence. Do you remember the good old days when common sense was a thing? Social distancing and masks are a daily embarrassment to science. HCQ, vitamin D3 and zinc are effective treatments for the covid cold but unplugging your TV totally cures it. We repeat for the sheep: how can there be roughly the same amount of deaths during a pandemic (2020) as before it? The only rational conclusion a sane person can come to is there is no pandemic.

Everyone who hasn't been brainwashed by covid propaganda must be a Jedi.

Have you noticed how nobody who speaks the truth catches covid. By deliberately removing people's personal identity and individual beliefs, our hierarchical nature gravitates towards reluctantly accepting cruel and disturbed figures of authority who exploit us instead of welcoming normal and fair people we want and deserve. Therefore our minds search for or create new, higher sources of leadership outside of and above this unrewarding and mercenary system which has failed our hearts and minds.

Many religions gave hope that altruism, kindness and friendly neighbourly attitudes were the future for mankind, but this hope for a better way is being rapidly eroded by globalist greed. Whether you believe in God or not, the world desperately needs Christian values to stop people losing their morals and minds. Furthermore, the only depopulation the world needs is of evil billionaires pretending to be God. I've picked my side. I'm on the anti-genocide team and it's confusing why we're a minority. Can you hold your head up high and say if the world was full of people like you the covid plandemic would have got nowhere?

They call it a safe vaccine, I call it a time delayed lethal injection. Potayto/potahto.

It's so heart-wrenching knowing that misguided anti-vaxxers who never wore masks either are all dropping like flies from covid because of their ignorance. But they're not are they. Not a single one. Quite the opposite dear sheeple. The covid vaccine is for ignorant people who don't know what's going on. Smart people avoid it at all costs. In 2021, millions of qualified doctors and nurses around the world refused to have the covid vaccine despite working near or with covid infected patients all day long. Therefore, something must be seriously wrong with that vaccine – some doctors preaching it's a bioweapon. If that doesn't wake the slowest of minds up, then the American Red Cross who always need blood donors DO NOT want blood from covid vaccinated people due to spike protein contamination and blood clotting. In 2020, when asked in an interview called Hold-Up what he thought about mass covid vaccination, recipient of the 2008 Nobel Prize in Medicine, Professor Luc Montagnier said,

"...It is an unacceptable mistake. The history books will show that because it is the vaccination that is creating the variants. For the China virus, there are antibodies created by the vaccine. What does the virus do? Does it die or find another solution? The new variants are a production and result from the vaccination. You see it in each country, it's the same: the curve of vaccination is followed by the curve of deaths... It is clear that the new variants are created by antibody-mediated selection due to the vaccination."

They might be trying to murder everyone, but looking on the bright side at least the self-righteous, deeply annoying people are going first. We're apparently in the middle of a pandemic but countries allow domestic and international flights to carry on spreading nothing around the world as usual. If there was a real pandemic, people would be fighting their way through crowds to get the vaccine, instead governments spend billions trying to persuade you. Moreover, if you accept mandatory vaccination you're whole life will revolve around big pharma's mandate until you no longer have a life. Mandatory vaccination is the same as governments giving you a ticket to ride the concentration camp train. Is it even a real or working vaccine if you need more than two shots? Calling the covid jabs vaccines when they vaccinate nothing is medical fraud and pure evil.

Many people very oddly didn't have any reaction/side-effects to the first two shots at all which makes conspiracy theorists wonder if the majority were saline instead to gain public trust. We could also question cold chain vaccine storage: one minute keeping the vaccines refrigerated was of upmost safety importance, then when they realised it was difficult to do on a large scale and there were nowhere near enough refrigeration units to transport and store billions of jabs around the world, they hardly mentioned it again. How many millions of deaths will it take before the sheep realise the vaccine is the pandemic. Parasites, nanotechnology, gene therapy and two poisonous words: graphene oxide.

Most people are very particular about what food they like to buy and eat but they don't give a fuck what's in a vaccine, which is very odd behaviour. They really have got the naive vaccinated believing the unvaccinated are prolonging this plandemic but if the vaccine really works why do the vaccinated give a fuck what anyone else does? The sheep will sell their own kids out just to go on a fucking holiday abroad.

Covid is the world's largest ever house of cards and just one gust of global truth could bring all the lightweight lies crashing down.

To summarize, lockdowns, masks and social distancing don't work and the covid PCR tests are 100% inaccurate (officially over 97% inaccurate). A healthy person who tests positive using an inaccurate testing process should not be counted as a medical case. A surge of covid cases either simply means loads of fucking idiots with nothing wrong with them got tested or much more likely the government statistics are incorrect. A US man tragically died in a car crash and his death certificate said Covid-19 killed him. Corruption is guaranteed by giving hospitals and doctors large financial incentives to record as many deaths as possible as *from* or *with* covid. If you find yourself in the unenviable position of being a decent person caught in the wrong job which now aids-and-abets tyranny in any small way, leave your job immediately because later in life your conscience won't be able to cash the cheques. Don't be a Stormtrooper, be a Jedi.

Any restaurant that tells unvaccinated people they're only good enough to eat outside like a dog on a leash can lose your business forever.

The covid vaccine doesn't stop you catching or passing on the alleged virus and after vaccine rollouts the death rate considerably increases (Israel has one of the highest vaccination tallies, yet frequently the highest amount of covid 'cases' and deaths *per capita*). The people profiting from the vaccine aren't liable for injuries caused and have given money to government scientists and media corporations. They're making untold billions from selling masks, covid tests and vaccines for viruses we already have herd immunity to whilst simultaneously taking over political power of virtually every country in the world under the guise of a faux global emergency. When you have unlimited money and own the world's media it's easily done. This is nothing short of a deadly medical fraud and *coup d'état* that millions of people are starting to wake up to, so without doubt they'll pull many new fictitious viruses and variants out of the hat, use numerous fake testing processes throughout this decade, then ramp up media scaremongering. As long as you know accepting the new normal will eventually end in slavery. Many hospitals are denying unvaccinated people vital treatments and lifesaving operations, illogically keeping ill people safe by allowing them to die. A few weeks to flatten the curve has become shooting at people losing their jobs in Australia. This isn't about a virus is it and never was. It's all going to kick-off big-time soon.

People who believe this is a real pandemic probably also think the money they donate to charity actually makes it to the victims. You're mentally ill and consumed by fear if you think stopping people from working or buying food for their family if they don't take an experimental vaccine has anything to do with a virus. The less you worry about catching a virus the less you are ill. As the poet and novelist Rudyard Kipling of The Jungle Book fame elucidates,

"Of all the liars in the world, sometimes the worst are our own fears."

spend a lot of time looking for dinosaur bones, lost civilizations and hidden treasures but haven't even bothered to put up a missing poster for the flu. The sheep will believe in this fake pandemic until the day they die which ironically is going to be much sooner than they think. The whole world is rapidly becoming like 1930's Nazi Germany with the unvaccinated playing the unenviable role of Jews. Vaccine passports are going to create a two-tier system: dead or alive. This is the only pandemic in history where people lose their jobs for helping.

> They simply wouldn't fire thousands of nurses during a real pandemic.

A very similar looking coronavirus (HCoV-229E) with the now familiar spike proteins was identified at the University of Chicago way back in 1962. For any scamdemic doubting Thomas' out there please prepare yourself for one final bombshell and clincher which proves beyond questionable doubt the Covid-19 pandemic is staged: a patent application for a system and method for testing for Covid-19 was first filed in the US on 13/10/2015 (patent no. US20200279585A1). How can you have a correctly named test kit for a disease which doesn't yet exist for another 4 years?

Furthermore, in 2021 the distinguished and meticulous Dr David Martin (expert doctor, PhD and inventor of an integrated laser system which targets and treats inoperable tumours) has only gone and blown the bloody doors off the global covid scam by revealing that,

"...The first vaccine ever patented for coronavirus was sought by Pfizer... which was specifically this 'S' spike protein — so the exact same thing that allegedly we have rushed into invention — the first application was filed on January 28, 2000, twenty-one years ago."

The general idea wasn't to flatten the curve but to flatten your spirit then bulldoze your life. When you get bullied by someone they slowly wear you down until you become used to being treated like shit as normal life. That's exactly what your government are doing to you now. You beat bullies by defying their demands and hitting them where it hurts. The New World Order completely underestimate how clever and resourceful the populace are which will be our saving grace. I sense the whole world slowly realising this is not about a virus anymore and wasn't from day one. Once you understand there is no covid virus and the people running the world are utterly ruthless you see the whole puzzle of evil and it all makes sense.

Based on the ancient story of Ahiqar (5th century BC in Elephantine) this meme perfectly sums up what's really going on,

"The forest was shrinking, but the trees kept voting for the axe, for the axe was clever and convinced the trees that because his handle was made of wood, he was one of them."

Big Brother is watching.

Liar, liar, pants on fire

We spend too much time looking at smartphones instead of the stars. In modern times, schools and mainstream media are significantly to blame for producing thoughtless zombies and brainwashed drones watching mindless dross and shocking lies on television. Journalists and editors can't even be arsed to mix crumbs of truth with their lies anymore and we're not even compensated with a feel-good panda story at the end of their globalist agenda news. If you actually believe what the news says your sheep level is hanging by its hooves in an abattoir. As much as you are attached to TV and mobile phones they're arguably the most psychologically damaging invention ever made. So why are we so obsessed with television beyond the obvious performing of life's highlights, attraction to good-looking actors and the social cohesion of talking points? It all comes down to wanting campfire community spirit again.

> It's not the truth just because the telly and radio says it about five fucking million times a day.

Real log fires not only look cosy and reassuring, with the occasional crackle to make you jump, they are one of the first phenomena in history which made us happy. Beyond their primary representation of heat, a full belly, light, safety and energy, fires also promote talking, singing and dancing among a wide circle of united friendships. Whatever loggerhead arguments, toils or torments village members struggled with during the day would all be negotiated, resolved and made-up around the fire before bed so everyone could sleep in peace. Fires build psychological bridges, imagination and make us see everybody else and the world in a different light. We are all heavily stressed by our paper-thin modern mortality and a fire reminds us of this. Aside from the entertainment factor, watching TV is addictive because it simulates the profound possibilities a fire gives you. Consequently, television has become the central method to conveniently push propaganda and buying opportunities to modify the masses minds. Mobile phone and app popularity works on a different principle which exploits your boredom and loneliness.

Television is the greatest hypnosis
the world has ever seen.

We are so chronically susceptible to media brainwashing that our whole society is based on bloody big lies orchestrated by really evil intentions. As a result we end up with the lowest common denominator of leader by allowing ignorance and cowardice to make decisions against our better judgment and the warnings your intuition transmits. Drumming fake, loud and flashing information into our heads minute by minute guarantees at least 3/4 of the world will defend the lies impregnated in their mainly subliminal minds. We should be seeking truth and wisdom through knowledge and experience, not via pop-up media entrapments and distractions. The real conspiracy theorists flick on the TV and listen to about 5-10 minutes of scaremongering sound bites without thinking which is apparently normal, whereas smart people spend days researching facts and figures to find out the real truth and get called mentally ill conspiracy theorists for their troubles. Sheeple really hate to see you live with pride. Determined and alert people work out the truth. Mentally weak and lazy people follow social narratives. If you're clever you don't just see out of the box, you burn it to fuel new ideas. Healthy debate creates a free society. Censorship is the road to tyranny. The vast majority of people will do whatever their government tells them even though virtually all politicians *never* have our best interests at heart. Most humans have good intentions, yet are submissive, chicken-hearted and can't quite believe the level of depravity leaders steep to. Congratulations to the rest of you who have a mind of your own and the spirit to survive!

The sheep need to realize that uncomfortable truths don't equal conspiracy theories.

Even worse than mainstream media and their adverse channels of transmission for indoctrinating the plebeians is the educational system which conditions impressionable young children to obey their master's rules without question under the guise of teaching, preparing kids to be hoop-jumping adult fodder for central banking syndicates. Generally speaking, teachers are the most brainwashed group you will ever meet whose job has become about limiting your child's mind so they give up on life before even leaving school, with rare inspirational exceptions who greatly improve growing and enthusiastic young thoughts. We want a world where our children question every single word their teacher's say, not an inflexible system where they get told off for not obeying programmed group consensus. A school's curriculum not only presents a biased representation of history but also becomes the perfect platform for the cult to flog millions of their tendentious books. More disquietingly, schools are rapidly becoming a sinister backdoor for the state to legally own your children if the adult doesn't conform to social dictates.

Schools are going to become one of the worst places for children to go.

If you want your child to be safe and learn well, homeschooling could be your best future option. The academic world moves at a snail's pace, always a couple of aping and plagiarising steps behind reality and the truth. Homeschooling is one of the best moves ever. You no longer have to battle with schools trying to control your kids but you'll learn loads yourself too and connect with your children more. Homeschooling is highly recommended for peace of mind and your children having a better education and well-being away from many disruptive children and an overall toxic school environment.

There's no point having schools and universities if virtually no-one ends up with a mind of their own.

Teaching his pupils to have a mind of their own didn't go well for Socrates. Anyone with brains who presents superior ideologies against the ruling classes' fiscal operations usually ends up another covid death statistic. People who call others a conspiracy theorist don't realize all societies are built on conspiracy. Most adults like to be told what to do and rarely evolve from their school playground mentally, so it's no surprise governments take advantage of us like abused children. It can be very frustrating how the asinine hoi polloi allow deranged despots to rule our lives without even batting an eyelid of defiance.

The powerful elite always seek to create a nasty world where everyone self-harms and only they sell the knives and plasters. If you can't accept that governments and their global business leaders *never* have your best interests at heart - especially including medical and retirement plans - then there's little hope for you so it's best you take the blue pill of pusillanimity and live a life of degrading servitude. This is a black and white choice you make for yourself, the family you love and everyone else in society who secretly hopes that mentally strong characters with dignity and pride will unite and ignite the power of the people.

Being a free thinker means you are exempt from believing lies. It has always been rich versus poor people and unless we start properly educating and edifying our minds with real information, research and thinking, rather than regurgitated, convenient falsehoods, we will always cower down to global bullies. Totalitarianism ends when we all pull the plug on the globalist's brainwashing empire.

The matrix is a place where they put you in a damp cardboard box and tell you it's for your own safety. The real world is you sitting up high on a tree branch enjoying a stunning red horizon. First they take away your freedom by making you dependent on money, then your pride by having to do a job you would rather not and then you become an accomplice to their artifice by pretending your low paid job has worth or status while they spend millions extravagantly. A feeling that what we do matters is part of our make-up to the point of making-up meaning even if it doesn't exist. Self-delusion produces a temporary easy feeling inside which later cements into a fear of change.

So how are modern humans going to fight their way out of the uneducated and brainwashed rabbit hole we find ourselves in? What can humans positively do to not be so sheep-like and childlike in their automatic levels of compliance? How do we learn to think for ourselves without being remotely influenced by society's cunning paradigm? To free your mind from the matrix you need to first become aware of yourself, then learn how the system deceives you and changes your natural behaviour. If you can't see how detrimental the system is you won't want to psychologically escape it. Self-awareness is the first small step for mankind. It takes real intelligence to assess your own behaviour objectively and then change for the better.

After you're done laughing at conspiracy theorists you can't believe you weren't one earlier.

Because global technology spreads information and trends faster than social media memes, humanity has entered a really negative, knee-jerk phase where people follow crowd consensus whether something is right or wrong and when they don't understand what's going on. Slaves who obeyed in the past did so under pain of death, but now people just willingly follow instructions without coercion or a single brain cell sparking up any pride inside their almost robotic mindsets. Most people think so little about anything it's a wonder they can even move their limbs without government guidelines. Subsequently, a great deal of us are under a common misconception that sheep and lemming-like behaviour is somehow inherent in our genes, blood type, testosterone levels or the generic human psyche, which isn't necessarily the case. There are common, contributory factors differentiating sheeple from free thinkers but how we become aware of our subconscious states is as varied as people are and everyone's level of *zanshin* (total awareness and continued state of spirit) is on a sliding scale. Humans are stuck in a strange stage of their evolution where most people use their intelligence to ignore their intelligence through fear they might become enlightened and realize they're living a lie.

The fear of social exclusion is far greater than the need to know the truth.

Sheeple put up little resistance against wolves, which allows evil to get humanity by the throat in a never-ending cycle of being sheared and slaughtered. Sitting there in fear and crossing your fingers whilst waiting for your number to come up isn't the way nature intended humans to live. If you're going to die by unnatural causes, do it on your own terms with a sword in your hand rather than being dragged out from under the bed.

We have caged our own species and walked away from our natural psychological homeland, leaving the inevitable consequences of slavery and mass slaughter – controlled democide – with inevitable extinction further down the line. The colossal population on the planet is not the problem. Not balancing and living in harmony with nature is. There is always a solution to every man-made trouble which doesn't require radical or oppressive methodologies. In addition, to ensure stability and peace, leaders need to be inspirational alphas you admire and want to follow, like Leif Erikson, Queen Boudica of the Iceni, Rosa Parks, Lady Æthelflæd of the Mercians, Alfred the Great, Joan of Arc and Harriet Tubman who was born into slavery, escaped and went on to make numerous missions to rescue approximately 70 enslaved people using secret routes and safe houses known as the underground railroad. Instead of real leadership with a moral compass, we always end up being led by spoilt brats who want revenge for being buggered at boarding school.

It used to be hard to tell if someone was mentally weak but now their flimsy mask shows you in broad daylight.

In nature, many predators scout-out for and can literally smell stress and illness. Subsequently, as well as obviously hiding and keeping a low profile, wild humans learnt to cover-up any weaknesses with short displays of aggression to fake it until they made it to a full recovery, or males even feigned sexual prowess to try and make themselves look virulent and *up for it,* so as to deceive the competition or enemy into believing they're not an easy target to pick on. Survival behaviours and courtship displays often involve posturing and bluffing.

A fair portion of stressed and on the edge modern men who sexually assault women fall into the same category as trying to display sexual readiness to mask their weaknesses. These desperate and confused individuals are not prepared to invest time and energy playing the dating game, deemed essential for testing a person's eligibility, mental strengths and social beliefs, so they resort to bypassing the courting/mating ritual altogether.

In days gone by such deviant behaviour would be dealt with swiftly with force or exile. For example, in old Eskimo tribes, if an alpha bully or sex pest murdered or kept assaulting a group member, one of the victim's family would arrange a secret meeting with other men from the tribe, sentence would be passed, they picked the man to do it and a fatal hunting trip was arranged. The perpetrator would most likely receive a deadly blow to his head when least expecting it or get stabbed in back and justice was served with raw fish. Strangely, the period between sentence and death could be a day to a couple of years, where the guilty individual continued to live within the tribe before randomly being executed. Perhaps that was the Eskimo's way of showing the group that lawbreakers will be tamed before their death to prevent others from committing crimes. Eskimos believe that too much thought leads to trouble, do not concern themselves with solving riddles and are content to not understand things. Our modern, over-thinking society could learn much from their practical, ancient ways. Small tribes aim for harmony and simplicity by uprooting evil and ostracizing anarchy, but in a mega-society the punishment rarely fits the crime because the law favours property over people.

People are past masters at both spotting and trying to hide weird and sexually repressed behaviour in a continuous social performance of outsmarting their rivals to gain one-upmanship and prestige. We are very cunning, sometimes sly and backstabbing, resourceful and always try to predict which way the herd is travelling next whether we follow them or not. Like it or not, most humans are outstanding liars because telling the truth often hurts their eggshell feelings. Ancient people used deceiving tactics to gain an evolutionary advantage, therefore it's no surprise that lying, the very thing which worked so well, is now the main course of decision making in a world full of people deceiving others to sell a product or concept beneficial to them.

Humans are so weird I advise you not to trust anyone until they prove their loyalty and then still remain cautious until you've had a damn good look into their soul.

Nowadays, a favourite tactic to disguise not pulling your weight is *busywork*, or many people use flirting to distract from their lack of productivity. Lying and believing lies is a massive human issue. We're programmed to believe, hoping it's a good opportunity, when most of the time we're walking into a carefully rehearsed trap. We are born into a social lie centred around greed. It's a hundred times harder to say *no* to our egocentric and materialistic society than to mentally escape a narcissistic relationship. Very few people are mentally strong enough to consciously pull the rug from under their feet to rebuild a better way of life against the grain of billions of sheep-like minds re-enforcing the controlled deceit. Bully victims always do as they are told. You only go with the flow when you don't know where to go. Vast hordes of nomadic minds are without anchor, oar or sail, drifting aimlessly towards rapids of compliance and a waterfall of debt.

The masses are always so far behind reality they're almost travelling back in time.

In contemporary society, comfortable lies are more popular than donuts. Humans even sugar-coat their mortality. No-one dies peacefully in their sleep. Death is a reminder to enjoy your life now and to not waste time on losers and liars. How do we even know anything is real other than pleasure and pain. Such is the immense power of media conditioning, the people who have been conditioned don't even know they have and take major umbrage at such a real suggestion. Consequently, society is brimful of fame seeking wannabes, fashion freaks trying to be someone they're not and hordes of striving blockheads who actually believe having a 4x4 makes you somehow superior, and even if it did, so what. We have all been guilty of showing-off like idiots at some point in our lives, only the sheeple make a permanent philosophy out of it and never work out what really matters until it's too late, and even then they'll deny the very existence of truth just like Peter did Jesus three times.

As individuals, sheeple have a total inability to see how their current behaviour affects the future and no surprise the collective lack of vision too. Most people will defend lies to the upmost heights and heavens until they lose their income and start to feel truly uncomfortable. Very few factors act as real catalysts to wake up the modern doltish mind to the frightening evil which currently steers human heads. Evil people usually hide out in charitable, religious or child foundations and describes themselves as global entrepreneurs, philanthropists or humanitarians, as the sheep applaud and revere them. Evil works hardest when you're enjoying your freedom. Only through adversity and trauma can you see the truth.

You're just a girl or guy, standing in front of a sheep, asking it to wake the fuck up!

Modern life has become so unnaturally comfortable that countless people have become uncomfortable with the lack of adversity and challenges faced. Puzzle making, stamp collecting and trainspotting have their limits. We are at our best and happiest when mentally and physically pushing forward to achieve fixed, necessary goals, followed by periods of calm reflection, generosity and family cuddles. Bone-idle behaviour and couch potato lifestyles have become our most popular sport because the big divorce from nature made millions of minds lack direction and meaning. Our schizophrenic society tries to break your spirit by pushing so many red and green light rules on you at the same time, it takes a big effort just to know where to start your journey and when to turn.

Let your spirit run like a fast flowing river as your freedom kayaks around rocks.

Whereas once guile and being cunning hunters protected and gained us opportunities, it has now developed into using our wits in a pointless system like wooden actors who can't remember their lines. Lying was a trap which caught food. Nowadays our double-dealing is just a hindrance to relationships and fair trade, causing much heartache and bankruptcy. Consequently, when modern people get very stressed and feel desperate they instinctually try to camouflage their odd and sometimes erratic behaviour by putting on a front instead of being honest and asking for help.

Running wild and free.

King of infinite space

To be free is life itself. As we have established, about one fifth of people are independent thinkers. That doesn't mean they won't readily conform if needs must, it just means they have a good appreciation of reality and know what's going on with society and the world. Free thinkers are more creative, honest, individual, recalcitrant and rebellious, significantly less fearful and much more visionary than sheeple. In contrast, the sheep like to think they are nice people but won't think twice about stabbing you in the back if it saves their skin, unlike free minds who often defend bully victims or sometimes become the wolf. Open minds are more honest about what's really happening in a situation. Without people who can think outside of the box, we remain trapped in a box. The matrix stops you being yourself and the sheep don't mind playing the contradictory, set role assigned to them. Free thinkers remain themselves from birth to death and are frequently boat-rockers. The world is a stage and the sheep willingly read out their lines whilst freethinkers write them. Being called a boat-rocker is a badge of honour you should wear with pride.

What the fuck is wrong with millions of Facebook twats casually trending shit about their hair and Kim Kardashian, blissfully unaware of the new holocaust creeping up behind them.

At what point does someone separate the organic embryo of their mind from the plastic sac of the matrix? Is there a great awakening or does awareness take baby steps? Are adults who don't feel comfortable being part of a group, different humans?

The level of uncomfortableness and anxiety sheep experience by not following the herd is similar to the collar pulling displeasure an outsider feels when forced to mix with the group. I put the *awakening* or mind and soul detachment from a corrupt system down to a person's natural ability to see and care about the great potential in humanity being wasted by greed and control, and this comes from having a positive mindset, seeing the bigger picture and wanting to do right by your fellow man and woman. And that trio of catalysts from an open mind usually happens before the child reaches 10 years old. All children are born with free minds which are usually very rapidly corrupted by their parent's failings and lack of foresight. Sheep produce lambs to the slaughter. Finding the truth comes from knowledge, thought and using your intuition. If you don't constantly read new material, have a think about what you believe and listen to your feelings, you'll be clueless to the triangle tones of reality. In chess, a clever pawn can promote itself to a powerful queen.

Freedom starts in your mind.

When adults wake up later in life, the trigger is almost always trauma, or a mental breakdown, or from a natural disaster, or tragedy. For adults to see the light there has to be a great change to reset their minds to a natural way of thinking. Many young children who are aware of the nefariousness of the matrix will feel caged by their lack of ability to change the situation or by having no-one to talk to about it who understands their mental claustrophobia. This lost black sheep feeling often causes children physical and mental illnesses such as asthma, eczema, rashes and allergies, genuine autism, panic attacks, social anxiety, depression, loneliness, autoimmune disease, migraines and even vertigo. These are natural reactions to a rotten society by a child who doesn't know how to fight back, deal with it or protect their feelings. An aware child is already awake without the revelation. An aware adult has likely had their curiosity tweaked by a major upset like a deceitful relationship break-up, or receiving shock medical news, so they start to question everything else too in a slow and difficult pigeon-toed path towards the truth. We don't question anything when it's going well, only when it's going badly. As adults we mostly unlearn what we already knew. A truly enlightened person never got convinced at any age that society was good for them and never felt part of the lie.

> Maybe the greatest human achievement
> is building a mind of your own.

Society is organised crime: you pay the bullies a slice of your profits and soul in exchange for protection from the elements, which ironically you were designed to live in. The sheep are experts at putting their head in the sand and pretending evil things don't exist. Why, because they are short-term thinkers who don't care about the future of humanity, only themselves. They'll do anything to uphold the status quo because a fight for survival scares them as they know they'll be killed first. The mentally and physically weaker people are, the larger the support network they maintain. Sheep are petrified of not being accepted by the crowd even when groups hurt them. Strong people stand alone and have many followers but few friends. We assume free thinkers know more, but sheeple know a lot more than they're prepared to let on or even admit to themselves. It all comes down to ignoring their intuition. The sheep deny their arboreal roots. They are more susceptible to being brainwashed and conned because their fear makes them mentally lazy. Sheep simply can't be bothered to delve into anything. Fear pins the people down and cowardice nails coffins. Also, it takes time and effort to fight your way out of the matrix. Why bother fighting a system you can't escape, think the sheep. Because a lie and scam is always worth fighting or there won't be a future worth having if we don't.

Your intuition is the heartbeat of life, the rhythm of the universe and not accepting the futility of it. Have respect for humanity's potential. Pride is very important. Free thinkers believe humanity can do much better and the sheep are afraid of change. Sheeple are negative, uncreative and don't like new information. They feel threatened by different ideas and obscure, abstract stimulus, whereas free thinkers welcome it and use their noodles much more. It's the process of discovery which enlightens you. The independent mind is nomadic and doesn't need holidays to feel happy. A sheeple's mind rarely goes anywhere so needs to literally plonk their inactive mind in a different location far away. Nearly everyone enjoys a holiday, but the sheep seem to almost have coronaries if they can't go away from the monotony they vehemently crave and defend like the walking paradoxes they are. The leaders make you play their economic slavery game and the repetition cons you into believing it's reality, but it's a construct carefully designed by lunatics who want a license to kill.

> Open-minded people don't mind being wrong.

It sounds harsh but the sheep are often creeps and liars, always scheming behind your back to avoid honest confrontation. Sheeple pretend to be nice and humble with their fake school parent smiles, but politely challenge their beliefs for a frank debate and a latent nastiness spits out venom like a cobra. They're not just blind with fear, they go out of their way to poke everyone else's eyes out too. Don't give up loving people just because the sheep are selfish. Sheep usually have fish-dead eyes and are happy to live a Truman Show lifestyle in exchange for superficial safety, which would be fine if they didn't ruin everything for the real people all the time by giving away democracy and rights without objection. Their ability to lie to themselves to reach some kind of psychological equilibrium is phenomenal, under the misinterpretation they're achieving safety. The first place people need to start a revolution is in their minds.

> Free thinkers are really good at reading the room. The sheep however, won't even read.

In direct contrast to sheeple, free thinkers make the world go round as much as love does because they create the freedom to love and for people to be themselves. They are simply not prepared to lie to themselves or be part of the cattle run to appease sycophants. Open minds look at the stars and see new worlds. They feel energy in wind and see voyages in rivers. Their minds are inherently positive, yet frequently downed by the sheer mass of package holiday makers who question nothing. Whereas the sheep want to be led, free thinkers look neither to be leaders or followers. They like to help guide humanity in the right direction and want to create a better world for everyone as well as themselves.

People who can't think outside of the box need to stay in their box and let open-minded people enjoy the fresh air.

A free mind is significantly in touch with its ancestral brain, listening to their intuition all the time and rejecting the addictive magnetism of a buy and chuck society. Detached thinkers appreciate that keeping up with the Joneses destroys your spirit because keeping up with yourself is hard enough. A key difference between the sheep majority and the minority of normal people is that sheeple frequently hate and even refuse to be criticized because retorts require effort, knowledge and confrontation. Alternatively, free thinkers don't mind or even relish lively debate or venting arguments and rarely succumb to peer pressure. In those rare times when critical thinkers join herd mentality they will hardly ever do so under pressure or coercion, but the opposite while feeling calm, choosing groupthink to make someone happy or because it happens to be the right move for once. Truthers are often curious types used to challenging their own discoveries and thinking, which is the whole point of mental development, to not remain set in your ways. They welcome as much new information as possible about all topics of interest and can occasionally become almost too open-minded, if there is such a thing, getting temporarily carried away and believing all information which contradicts staid, profiteering narratives. Sometimes open minds don't know when to close them.

Most differently, the sheep defend the small shed of family philosophies they've had passed down from their parents until the day they die, rarely exploring life outside the boundaries of their own mental territory. Sheep don't want to face their mortality, so create a chain store mentality with as many safe zones as possible. Essentially, sheeple reject natural living in favour of being the rich man's badly treated pets in an experimental zoo because thinking stresses them out and makes their wool stand on end. Being a critical thinker is mainly down to a person's thirst for knowledge and truth.

It doesn't matter if I'm surrounded by rough seas of ignorance, I'll still keep boating along with the truth powering my sails.

Thinking about what unsavoury, despicable and reprobate things wealthy evil people do, especially to children and even babies, doesn't lighten anyone's party mood. However, free thinkers acknowledge the deepest and darkest fathoms of evil our society hides in high places, whereas sheeple always turn a blind eye to the powerful establishment. If you don't recognize evil and do your little bit to fight it, then you have no idea what side of the fence you're on. Sheeple are afraid to discover their white picket fence has a stray wolf in the back garden. Ultimately, they can't bear to think about evil and particularly the morbid subject of death. They're afraid of the unknown, the afterlife and hate the idea there may be complete nothingness after dying. The fear of death kills life.

Free thinkers accept death and get on with their lives. The sheep are absolutely petrified of dying. That's the fundamental difference between seeing the truth and being compliant without question.

Most collapses of a country's standard of living are deliberately manufactured, but we are always led to believe it was unavoidable. In brief, the powers that be use an age old, tried and tested trick of sinking the economy into debt by deficit spending whilst injecting non gold standard paper money which produces hyperinflation. Then they buy up all the properties at dirt cheap prices and later down the line stabilize the economy again to become filthy rich landowners. Another well known political tactic is creating trade blockades, sanctions and embargoes against a country that doesn't play ball, destroying their economy, then taking the land and buildings off them at a pittance before inserting a new leader who represents the world's central banks. Many nations who don't co-operate are accused of terrorism or harbouring terrorists. Currently, the level of worldwide personal debt is frighteningly high. In effect, if you owe them, they will own you, especially in a cashless, social credit score society.

Were it not for brave and psychologically strong people, humans would be stuck in a rut of real, perpetual slavery. Nowadays, there simply aren't enough awkward and dangerously stubborn people prepared to get wheeled off in a straightjacket to defend their principles. Many people are full of despair and a foreboding feeling of powerlessness.

History is a repeating cycle of the same wealthy families and cults trying to enslave the poor and every time the people won out it's because they stuck together and believed it was possible to win. Spartacus may have lost the Gladiator War against Crassus in 71 BC, after many previous victorious battles, but his glorious defeat improved slave conditions and changed laws, eventually paving the way for rebellion, inspiring hundreds of thousands of future slaves and foreign tribes to take down the mighty Roman Empire.

> Bravery is an underrated
> sign of real intelligence.

Strong minds don't accept defeat as an option. Free thinkers often display a cast-iron willpower and unwavering determination to never submit to the forces of evil. They rarely give up or submit to coercion because they know they're right. A very positive mindset keeps their spirits high and always finds a way out of difficult problems or trouble. When you lose hope you also lose the solution to your predicament. The free mind has a natural ability to re-orientate itself away from social traps, brick wall thinking and emotional blackmail because it knows where it's going. A really independent thinker has without doubt endured fairly long periods of the monk on the mountain type solitude in their life. You can't prize your mind away from society's virtual contrivance without a healthy separation from its working routine. To reject society is to understand it. The sheep never go off the well beaten track which is why they never find the truth. Open minds feel naturally sickened by our sick societies, but sheeple support the sickness like idiots fanning a fire in their own home.

If you ask a sheep why they're really doing something they rarely know why.

Free thinkers usually feel uncomfortable being told what to do and are therefore very difficult to bully. They would make great leaders but don't really like mixing with the sheep because it interrupts their focus and drags their energy down. They also often have a no nonsense, no bullshit approach to life which never fully accepts the 9-5 procedure even if that's what they have to do to survive. Naturally, free thinkers often go to bed way past midnight and wake up very late, or vice versa following a farmer's up with the sun, early to rise, early to bed practicality. Society's paradigm is simply way too boring for a free mind who feels restricted by its unnecessary and petty, hoop jumping complexity, not wishing to get bogged down in red-tape and red light rules. Some adults just become fed-up with it all and transcend the society treating them like stupid children. For example, giving fully grown humans a sticker to show they've had a vaccination really is contemptuous, especially not offering a lolly too. Free thinkers are slightly more likely to mentally snap during peace time but much less likely than the sheep to crack during real emergencies like war or a fire in a building. On the contrary, during highly stressed times the open mind comes into its element whilst the sheep freeze like rabbits in headlights. A free soul can even relish war time and often looks for opportunities to be a hero. The free thinker typically carries an air of anarchy, healthy cynicism and an underlying wish for revolution.

> Perhaps it's time to go back
> to the trees and start again?

An open mind will also always gravitate towards nature. A love of nature shows you haven't got caught up in economic barbwire and that your prehistoric brain remembers what it was like to be free and wholly responsible for your own destiny. As much as we crave community, we also need a sense of individual wellness and an opportunity to understand who we are, feeling both oneness and togetherness which must be practiced away from the herd. You don't become a real adult until your mind has gone walkabout for a number of months, living off the truth of the land. Nature represents the uncorrupted truth without conceit, distortion or control.

Without any nature to escape into, life could be perpetually depressing. Being with nature makes you feel alive and refreshed. It's naturally brighter outside and this immediately lightens your mood. When the sun shines on your face you are without worries in those blissful moments. And on a dusky sunset beach as the tide goes out, your energy is drawn towards the ocean and you can forget the bullshit life of buildings and banks behind you. The sea is a romantic reminder that you are better than what society says you are and there is more to life than a limiting narrative. Our greatest dream is living in harmony with nature.

A walk in the woods alone with
sunlight passing by leaves is
what everyone really needs.

Nature reflects the best version of you and restores lost energy. The oceans rejuvenate your spirits and forests get you in touch with your feelings reconnecting you to ancient psychology and healing. Just walking on grass in bare feet, grounding or earthing, connects you to the Earth's surface electrons which can boost your immune system as well as many other health benefits.

The great outdoors is a binding force for good which should *be* our lives, rather than an add-on. Trees will absorb your tears and storms can electrify your ambitions. Clouds give you perspective and mountains inspire the awe you need to believe in heavenly forces. Being with nature is paradise on Earth and your best opportunity to feel positivity flow throughout your consciousness. Aside from seeing your children happy, there's nothing better in this world than watching an orange sun go to sleep for the day and feeling it's energy pass to you. We often forget how much a short stroll in a park reinvigorates your soul.

The idea of living in a wood cabin far from our gas and politically polluted society becomes more appealing every day.

Nature

Panda blues.

Water, shapes and light

The blue of a Ulysses butterfly even betters a clear blue sky. So what makes us complex humans satisfied with life? How do we like to live? What do people really need to survive happily? Does nature provide the answers?

> Early morning birdsong reminds you how precious life is.

Whether you are religious or not, we all have the inherent idea that some form of returning to nature feels right. That's because cities are not fulfilling our water-based and visual needs as well as our natural emotional attachments. Trees and plants hold vast amounts of water and we like to be surrounded by the energy and shapes these provide. Approximately 60% of an adult's body weight is water so naturally our walking minds synchronise with running water. And our eyes, your primary sense for survival, feel very comfortable in leafy, camouflaged settings. Beyond the obvious, all of your visceral, earthborn senses are connected to the wild in a never-ending relay of spiritual and intuitive messages all singing from the same subconscious hymn sheet. Take a leap of faith and I'll take you to a valley where wild flowers grow.

Nature is our number one fantasy. Content minds need 3 main elements from the great outdoors: to be surrounded by the energy of water, organic shapes and patterns, and to absorb sunlight as a symbol of hope and new life. Bringing a natural setting indoors via décor or a pond-like mindset is very important. When choosing art, over 9 out of 10 of us love a healthy and honest landscape picture hanging up at home or on your computer wallpaper, especially displaying trees, water and the sky. And city landscapes most favoured have lots of lights streaming or beaming, representing the sun's rays and warm blood within. Hand painted, original art are attempts to recreate reality mixed with emotions, therefore are an excellent measure of what kind of truth and reality people seek. Studying a cross section of artistic styles and content over the centuries we observe the same well trodden natural themes and passions.

We see beautiful greens and sea blues, calm lakes and their ripple shapes, leaves aplenty, criss-cross branches meeting like lovers, luminous green moss, dramatic clouds, vast space, paths meandering, a womb cave suggestion, some mountainous rock and hills, a collaboration of nice pinks and friendly yellow reflections, sunset and sunrise oranges, red ember glows, snow covered soft white and heavy trees, green grasses, bridges over water leading to somewhere mysterious, holes in jagged rocks, layers in mud, wave energy and waterfalls, beams of holy light, shadows and silhouettes, and most loved of all is a clear blue sky.

Make a love of nature the catalyst for change and the template for your reasoning.

Water and sunlight are the foundations of life and only a small percentage of people get to enjoy enough of either. It is often remarked we live in a grey, flat pavement, unfeeling environment. A slate looking society which makes lots of people very depressed. We sweep nature away to lay down sombre slabs everywhere and then spend a lot of time visualizing beautiful holiday locations. It's a kind of madness akin to a drug addict taking drugs to help them stop taking drugs. City living is just not doing it for most of us. Humans are holding ourselves in aesthetic and emotional limbo by living in pedestrian, urban landscapes. Most buildings are vapid right-angled constructions (right-angles are incredibly rare in nature, mainly found in crystals). We sit on top of nature in cuboid high-rises dividing greenery up into disconnected islands. A tarmac, materialistic civilization is not sustainable and will face hard times to survive like this in the future.

In pleasing contrast, nature provides inexhaustible variety, colours and daily new growth. There's a continuous ebbing and flowing of wondrous textures and millions of organisms. You'll never even know the tip of the iceberg about nature's designs and facts. Did you know that adult females in buffalo herds vote on which way to travel by each looking in a particular direction, then laying down again, one vote at a time. Or that Greenland sharks can live up to roughly 500 years old, or that miniscule sea plants called phytoplankton produce at least half of the world's oxygen. The wilderness is awe inspiring, powerful and cyclic, and we become unhappy if its not part of our daily routine. Being removed from nature doesn't stop an instinctual yearning to return.

Depression is caused by many factors (relationship break-ups, redundancy, bad parental guidance, bullying, abuse, etc) and money worries are the top cause. Yet beyond these real-life pressing concerns underlying all of our personal troubles, is the split which modern people made from woods and water. The bones of history are littered with civilisations gone to the dogs for centralising their population too densely. For example, the very cruel yet advanced Mayan civilization of over 19 million people collapsed sometime during the 8th and 9th centuries due to over-logging and a lack of cloud water, because deforested land sponges up less solar radiation.

About 71% of the Earth's surface is covered in water, but less than 0.01% is fresh surface water in rivers, lakes and swamps. Water is sacred to Hindus and Anamists believe water has agency and is alive, helping to connect people together. Some people even believe water has a memory, but that homeopathic theory has proven false. Nevertheless, water is one main reason we are alive, holding moon energy with our life force floating around it. Water seems magical in clouds, becomes reflections across rivers, talks through streams and also helps wash away the sins of Man.

> If you don't mind getting wet
> you don't have to run from the rain.

Our societies have evolved far quicker than our brains care for and this leaves lots of people confused and vulnerable. So we seek solace in vices; socializing, organised fun centres, hobbies, quiet time in parks for lunch, or travelling around the world, when we should just be living in a healthy natural setting all the time in the first place. Humans destroy the nature around us and then replace the need for it with bad simulations and unsatisfactory alternatives. Cities pollute your mind even more than your lungs. Returning to the trees would make us much happier. Nature provides all of the interest, relaxation and colour a person would ever need.

If we start again with small villages full of groups of familiar people living off the land, then we'd be all-set for a satisfying life without mobile phones. Our safety seeking minds prefer to live in small, comfortable sized log cabins in a community of roughly 300-500 people near an umbrella of trees and fresh running water. Small towns were built on swapping friendly smiles. It's very important to be friendly, but more important for nature to befriend you.

Mother Nature's hair is like warm rain flowing down a window, her eyes mirror the blue moon and her mind is pure like a fresh running stream.

Contemporary citizens have become mundane and pliable, almost like cattle. We are herded from one place to another on the clock. Waking the sheep up is as difficult as finding a hibernating hedgehog. Being forward-eyed predators we should cope well with the challenge of fear and fighting, so acting like sheep feels incongruent. In the wild it was always *real* fear, not the fear itself of the unknown fear. Humans have badly controlled their gathering tendencies, creating envy, misplaced confidence and an overall lack of balance which causes in-fighting.

Monetary practicalities dominate society in every last decision and that is bad news for happiness. Corporations have done their best to supply us with as much rubbish we don't need and also excel at motivating frenzied and pressured buying opportunities which have no intrinsic benefit. None of this aimless avarice has made humans remotely happy. A disgruntled and dissatisfied feeling hovers over every purchase we make, whether we know it, like it, care about it, or not. Buying things makes you unhappy in the long run. It's a game of cat and mouse you play with your mind's desire, which usually ends in misery. No sooner has the elation of an excited purchase turned into a tiny-slump of emotions, followed by the need for another scouting and buying fix. Shopping is addictive, but more than that, global organisations are tapping the essential sap of our souls by preying on our survival instincts.

Financial markets exploit us, whereas nature is bountiful and pacifies our desperate grasp around greed. Why strangle the quality of generosity because giving makes you feel better. Breaking ourselves of the need to constantly buy stuff is one of the first major steps to re-connect properly with nature. In life, many people will let you down but nature always supports you. Our minds are stressed and homeless in frenetic cities. Nature is our true ancestral home and she will always welcome you with open arms and birdsong.

In warm April showers your mind expunges
highs and lows of rainbow glows to
a bright future of colourful shows.

Nature has had us on the run for most of our existence and slowly, step-by-step, humans have tamed the wild beast by eradicating, not harmonizing. A great fear is we may only wake up when it's too late to reverse the damage. Genetically modified crops could be an uncontrollable scientific spiral into anti-diversity, upsetting the natural balance of our worldwide ecosystem.

We have evolved into natural guardians of the planet and are doing a terrible job. Either we start protecting less capable species or end up ashes of our own making. All evidence supports a great rethink and rebuild of our living landscape for the good of mankind. Cities are good for business but bad for emotions. We are not where we want to be, but dolphins are. How crazy is a race which imprisons itself.

Why can't we just have nice leaders who
hand out fresh bread and cakes to the people
instead of pesticide food and deadly vaccines.

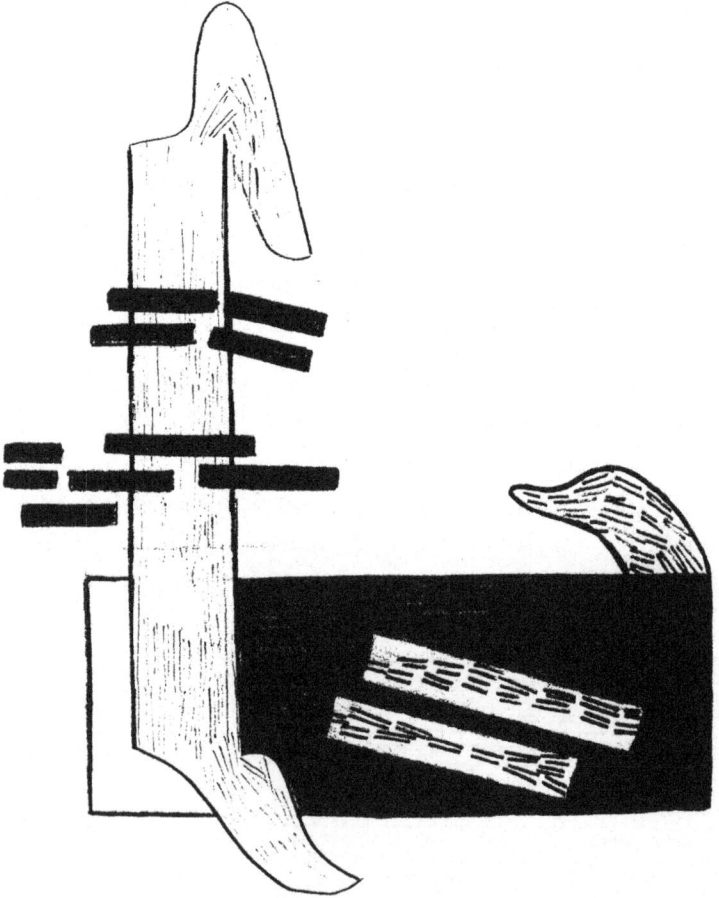

Granite and sea.

Rock glory in caves

You were born to be creative, not a 9-5 automaton. Many archaeologists and evolutionists say that *Homo sapiens,* us, are the last remaining human species in a long line of *Homo*'s (including *Homo - erectus, habilis, ergaster, georgicus, antecessor, neanderthalensis, denisovan, heidelbergensis, rhodesiensis,, rudolfensis* and *naledi*). The exact number of human species' could be up to and over 21, but is unknown and hotly debated. One particularly interesting archaic human species called *Homo floresiensis,* nicknamed the 'hobbit', stood about 1.06 metres high (3 ft 6 in) and used to hunt pygmy elephants (*Stegodon,* now extinct) and Komodo dragons.

Studying our recent human ancestors we understand how wrong it is to commonly misinterpret these kin as stupid or backward compared to us. Neanderthal adults weren't only significantly stronger but also had larger brains than city humans and created some of the most exciting, innovative and profound art that humans have ever produced. In fact, I would hazard a guess that modern cave men and women were marginally smarter and much more capable than us contemporary folk because their lives had real urgency and purpose. We have in some respects mentally de-evolved.

Inheriting an acceleration of technology in a comparatively short space of time has given us a false sense of superiority over our ancestors who invented the building blocks of Civilization. Lethargic lifestyles and eating McDonalds for many doesn't help cognitive functions and encourages children to use tablets whilst shovelling salty and sugary shit into their mouths. The corporate brainwashing starts early. Kids don't need junk food or play centers. They need parks, sunshine, fresh air and nature, otherwise they become accountants.

Hiking across countryside reconnects you to our nomadic roots and breathes fresh sanity into your lungs and mind again.

Your mind has craved the apotheosis of Mother Nature since time immemorial. We observe in prehistoric cave paintings the same drives, motives and intentions to impress that modern people have. In awe of the striking aesthetics we are equally taken by how well beliefs travel in time. Also, we see the perfect fat, bone and charcoal binding of humanity's fundamental need to communicate with nature, ourselves and higher beings.

Our basic minds haven't changed much in about 40,000 years or more. Just like small modern African or Papa New Guinea tribes, prehistoric humans always viewed animal sacrifice in a celebratory and symbiotic relationship with nature - being part of it, not above it. No doubt life was brutal, but Neanderthals and *Homo sapiens* still had the time and energy to make beautiful spiritual art in caves they mostly didn't inhabit. Exploring caves and past human lives is a great way to find a deeper meaning and gain perspective.

Parietal art (cave art) used natural earth pigments mixed with spittle or animal fat, giving cave paintings a visceral edge canvas and wood panels can't compete with. They are raw, powerful, meaningful, without pretension and profound. Animals were their main source of inspiration. They also showed hunters, hands, weapons and an infrequent painted tree; wiped, flicked or blow-sprayed (through hollow bird bones) onto carefully chosen sections of rock.

It's funny when archaeologists painstakingly spend weeks reconstructing a clay bowl the original owner didn't give a shit about.

Prehistoric tribes were very thoughtful, using all manner of ways to psyche themselves into a stupor so they could understand and prophesize nature's way. They tried to touch the hand of God by using all resources available to help them feel at home with their souls and influence the outcome of a hunt. Hunting rituals gave rise to higher thoughts bringing the pack closer, unifying the whole group's aims to track, find and end the life of another mammal for survival. By using every part of the animal, even ground bones for white paint, the tribe paid homage and gave respect to their life-giver.

Most cave art is figurative with spiritual elements mixed in: these were realistic nomads looking for an edge to bring down their prey. Cave art was the first signs of science and religion combined, perhaps seen as seminal early churches or art galleries. A love for nature and art connects you to the power of your ancestral roots.

Real art that has something worth saying needs to make a comeback.

Did prehistoric hunters want and expect their art to be seen beyond their lifetime; we guess so. Were these images the first type of bibles; probably. Cave art found by other conquering tribes must have added a lot to their own culture and hunting ways. Even in simply practical terms, the paintings gave a helpful shopping list and map of the game available to hunt in that area.

The large variety of creatures depicted in cave art around the world includes; bison, horses, cave bears, reindeer, bulls, eland, rhino, elephants, ibex, aurochs, woolly mammoths, cave lions, panthers, musk ox, ass, anoas (dwarf buffaloes), saiga, chamois, wolf, fox, red deer, wild boar, hare, otter, antelopes, hyenas, warty pigs, seals, catfish, cows, reptiles, birds, mullet, sabre-toothed felines, giraffes, Tasmanian tigers, crocodiles, capybaras, ostriches, moose, woolly rhinoceroses, guanacos, rheas, polar bears, snake-necked turtles, monkeys, cattle, domesticated dogs and humans. But no complete landscapes at all in Upper Paleolithic art (Late Stone Age, roughly 50,000-12,000 years ago), just a few stick type trees. Cave artists also painted comparatively few portraits unlike our self-obsessed, selfie generation.

Contrary to most art today, cave art sought to expand their minds and understanding of the world to connect with higher plains of reality, creating mythology and exploring supernatural possibilities. In the Cave of Swimmers in the Libyan Desert part of the Sahara, a series of floating figures adorn the walls and some look mysteriously like mermaids. On the Indonesian island of Sulawesi, a very old hunting scene depicts some part-human, part-animal figures known as therianthropes; one character wearing a tail and another hunter displaying a bird's beak. At *Grotte di Fumane* in North Italy and *Grotte Chauvet*, southern France, we can see a horned bovid with a human body and bison-man astride a lion woman. The famous cave art therianthrope at *Trios-Frères* in south-west France, known as The Sorcerer, depicts a fascinating mixture of a stag, an owl, a wolf and a human, but the well-known sketched interpretation by archaeologist Henri Breuil is a little bit suspect, leaning his striking artistic style towards his theories. Nevertheless, by studying the genuine animal and human hybrid representations from all those years ago, it's obvious that humans will do anything to find out who they are, where they came from and what they were born to do.

In the dark times coming your love
for the truth will be tested way beyond
your comfort zone and how much light
is left shall reveal who you really are.

In the depths of cave worship we connected with our deep unconscious mind, conjuring mythical beings, supernatural desires, shapeshifters and spirits, magicians, shamanic rituals and fiends from folklore. We nurtured our phenomenal imaginations and possibly created the origin of religious thought now innate in our mindset, unable to fully amputate even by the most cold and cynical of thinkers. Whether or not early humans literally grew god in their minds like the caves grew cave popcorn, or whether they developed the most direct and powerful way of finding God is still intensely debated. Perhaps shamans took advantage of their elevated status and power, corrupting their knowledge for selfish gains and thus started the whole process of religious corruption stealing the word of God.

The rock itself acted as the backdrop so their focus was on the animal's strengths and habits. The painting and worshipping process was a hand into the rock journey beyond one's own mind, welcoming new knowledge, albeit potentially frightening. Cave painting was brave of them, like a journey into uncharted waters or underground rivers, but unlike us, early hominids were used to being very brave. Our species has a real desire to hide deep down concepts and themes of interest, even bury to protect like the Egyptian pharaoh's tombs and secret crypts. We want our lives to be eternal and without vain.

> The contemporary art world is nothing more than a tax free way to launder billions of dollars.

The Impressionist painters delivered aesthetics so right, some to pure perfection like Monet's water lilies, but cave artists got it much more spot on. They were the first marks of art, therefore the most genuine gestures. And about three quarters of those finger dabs and smudges which made this astonishing work were female. Rock art was not only a good-luck spiritual exercise and attempt to better themselves, but a way to increase their vocabulary. Paleoarcheologist Genevieve von Petzinger catalogued 32 repeated symbols in Ice Age cave art, including negative and positive hands; asterisk; finger flutings (parallel lines); penniforms (branch/feather-like); tectiforms (hut constructs), which were repeatedly painted by Early Modern Humans in Europe around 30,000 years ago. The solid walls were their dictionary and spiritual decoration, library and hope.

Modern art nowadays seems more about getting away with having no skill than a need to explore the unknown.

Cave art shows you that testing your mettle, finding your inner self and bringing those basics to bear in the world is deeply important for balancing with nature. From the outset our species has presented huge problems for all other mammals by evolving more efficiently; hands gripping trees is the winning survival formula. From the very beginning our place and conscience in nature's pecking order has been in question. The beautiful cave art is a stunning celebration of our success and a psychological guide to our modern lives too. These foundational scratches into high contrast colourful expressions are walls of uncorrupted prophecy. We can also see why shopping has become so popular.

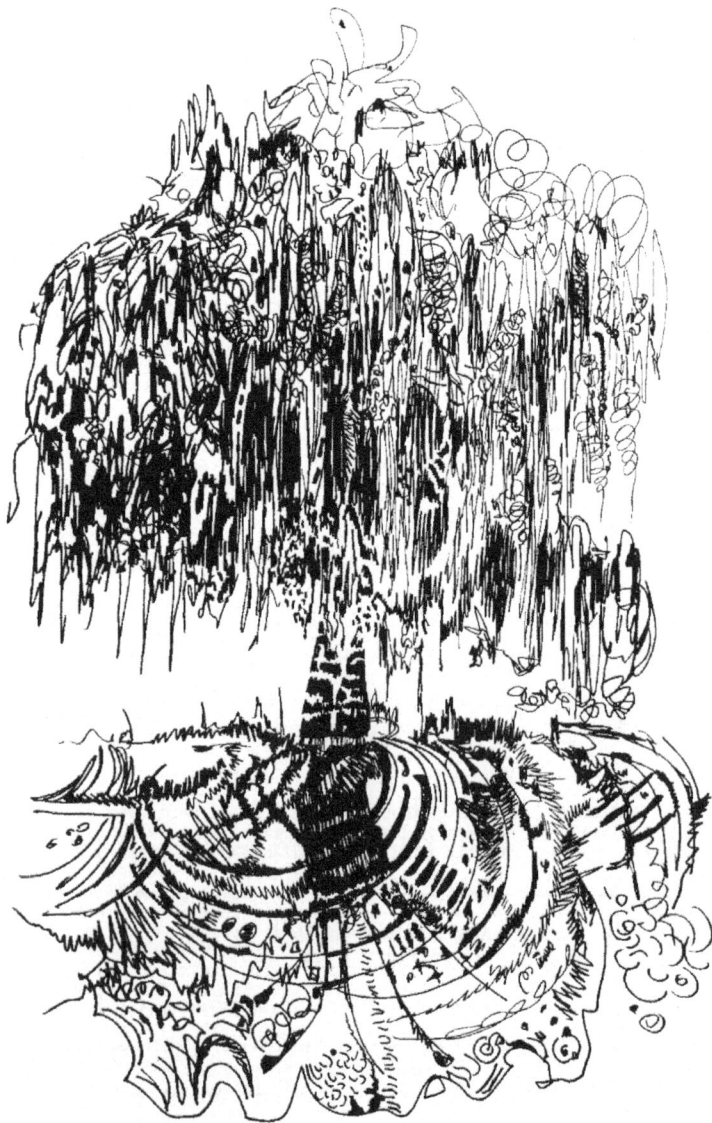

Belle of the ball.

The Totem of Trees

A walk in the woods does wonders for your well-being.
Humans are an extension of trees as they have always
supported us one way or another. Our nimble hands are
perfect for climbing branches to reach safety, picking leaves
and fruit. Trees are just about the coolest growing nature
around. Imagine life without trees.

When's the last time you climbed a tree?

Anthropologists say our adroit swinging and sleeping in
trees for protection eventually made our common primate
ancestors (*Ardipithecus* or Australopithecines) formidable
enough to gradually come down from the trees about 4
million years ago and explore the plains. I don't think we did
climb down from trees in evolutionary terms, nevertheless
our body's nerve structure looks very tree-like and we've
always had a close affinity with trees and wood, which is
such a beautiful looking material to sculpt and enjoy.

Trees were the hub of societies once. People commonly made
log cabins and warmed themselves by embers. Its incredible
versatility, patterns and hardiness make wood probably the
most used material throughout history; crafting arrows,
houses, tools, flooring, furniture, boats, fences, toys,
instruments, etc, and even clogs. Wood has a friendly
quality which metal and glass do not. A solid wooden table
almost seems to have soul. The dull hollow sound of wood-
tapping reverberates honesty into us. We are like leaves on

a tree all searching for the most light in our lives. Depressed people are drawn to peaceful parks full of green grass and an assortment of native trees because they are known to lower cortisol, a stress hormone. Our immune system gets tired of repugnant pre-fabricated greys, always welcoming trees as a reminder of freer days as symbols of safety from predators and the harsh elements. Trees seem to have a great capacity to absorb our problems. Also, the bouncing back-and-forth cheerful sounds of many birds in the trees is an essential part of the relaxation and healing process that woods provide.

The central heartwood supporting pillar of a tree is in many ways as strong as steel and the other surrounding 4 fibrous layers of wood each have different functions and densities, making them a natural cushion for our anxieties (the outer bark, phloem, cambium cell layer, then heartwood). If you think this is doubtable, next time you're upset, put the palm of your hands on any tree trunk for a few minutes and try denying it didn't make you feel slightly better, detached and grounded. You will feel the surface bark's resilient texture and sense its water and energy inside. A forest presents the perfect setting for a good cry.

There's no moonlight without sunshine in your life.

Hospital recovery rates improve when a patient can see trees outside their window and in 1984 the behavioural scientist Robert Ulrick also proved that fewer doses of pain medication were needed too. Trees are the perfect barometer for understanding our feelings, serving as an instrument to appreciate your misfortune and progress. We feel at home with trees around us. They are an anchor point, protection from the rain and will most likely be there many rings of time after you are gone.

> Watching a sunrise is what
> optimism is all about.

In bow-tie formation, trees sit into a perfectly married balance of growth, in unison above and below ground. What they take from the earth and sun, they return in full honour. Trees are honest and unlike humans when they proliferate, little is worse off for their success – quite the contrary growing in balance with the sun and wind. Giving so much life and air to the world, we must not underestimate trees' importance to our existence and the well-being of this planet. Each tree is a totem to life, the more the better. They grow like us (spinal column and trunk to brain canopy) yet with a freedom to expand beyond a body's limits. Trees seem timeless and reliable. Plant one anywhere you like, follow its gradual progress throughout your life and your problems are put in perspective. Holding evolutionary intelligence, people always desire to be near and around trees. Trees are our best friends and dogs like them too.

> The more I understand humanity,
> the more I respect oak trees.

Sacred heart.

Architecture of life

Homes used to be designed around the fireplace, now it's the TV. So if it's best for people to be surrounded by trees and water as the rootstalk of good human health, how is this possible in an industrialised computer age, especially when rabbit hutch architecture already dominates? We obviously can't change what has been, but we can ignore mistakes and rebuild new, better areas, forsaking the concrete stacking block society and mindset. Only about 3% of the world's land surface has been urbanised. We tower over each other, casting shadows of social mania. The greenbelt and forests are widespread, so why not try to turn them into new natural living quarters in an interactive and coalescent way?

In such a cruel world,

make your home a safe place to relax.

Humanity is currently like an overly pushy parent ruining their child's self-esteem and future for their own *stressed-out* selfish needs. Global companies are the bullies promoting a *buy-and-chuck* society and us honest citizens are their environmental victims. Most of us want to do the right things and this goodwill is taken advantage of by a nasty mouthful of murderous M's; manipulative, misguided and megalomaniacal moguls. Consequently, many people turn to God to find some peace and salvation away from an unforgiving artificial setting built by economic dictators. By coming together to find meaning, religion provides real camaraderie and very comforting emotional support. However, almost all religious teachings oppose modern greed which is hard to shy away from when money talks. Ancient words of wisdom commonly preach detachment from the ills of covetousness and greed, which paradoxically is the nub of the society we virtually all live in. How can you be in the world and not a partial slave to its financial scheme. Nevertheless, no tribes have ever existed without having their beliefs twisted or challenged by technology and progressive influences. Religion removes turmoil, provides a much needed sense of local community and offers valuable hope when decent help is in short supply. Having faith without feeling the need to prove your faith is a strength in itself. Critics could argue that by segregating in a religious huddle from the mainstay of thoughts and ephemeral crazes, we allow ourselves to enter a state of promised happiness which falls short of the broad-mindedness and supreme knowledge we should be seeking.

If there is a God he probably kicks himself daily wondering why he ever bothered.

Other people see the logical process of science as a counterbalance to the control governing them. Believers in science are drawn by the explanation of truth in tangible and microscopic forms. Yet some feel lost and lonely in a vastly unimaginable universe. A strong belief in one's self and neighbourhood teamwork could help bridge the two lifetime antagonists of religion and science, but humans need more than that. They need to feel like there is something much greater than a worker ant mortality. We want to know there is hope of life after death and our life wasn't all for nothing, even if it means possibly making it all up in our heads. Is belief without science a type of delusional mental illness or is trusting a continuously evolving subject like science just foolish? Anything that helps you through the trials of life is generally very good. Our souls could be our god, but it is in our nature to look to the heavens, not within ourselves. The wide sky is more appealing than deep oceans. A positive and effective extension of thoughts of goodwill is to worship Mother Nature and let her do what she has been doing very effectively for millions of years. We are not even a newborn in her cradle of time and nature shall overgrow our impatience to find meaning in life.

Living in awe of Mother Nature's wonders is what life is all about.

For once, human progress would be to go backwards into the dense forests of old. What is the point of taking away a person's manual purpose with computer controlled devices when using our hands naturally makes us happy. For well over 300,000 years modern people's brains have developed and worked responsively in tandem with evolutionary demand. But since industrialization started to really take off in the 1800's, society has moved at an alarming and detrimental pace. Ergo, depression and anxiety cloud over so-called progress. Technology should be used to help us, not entrap our lives further by making exploitation easier in an austere system. Very little technology is helping us mix with the world. Rainforests are being cut down nearly as fast as social morals. A powerless, foreboding feeling has become the staple diet of our inactive group mentality. Many greatly optimistic attempts and confused charitable enterprises gave people the feeling that positive change is around the corner. This false hope is naive and often preached by egotistical entrepreneurs masquerading as modern day prophets. Humans have a bad habit of distributing the numerous funds of good intentions and grand ideals to their limited liability companies. Large parts of the world still live without fresh running tap water and slavery is in full swing after decades of big donations. This is the true and sad state of things. Our environment has to dramatically change before our behaviour follows suit. Humanity is obsessed with worshipping money. In Britain, money worshippers are more common than Chicken Tikka Masala.

Humans spend a lot of time wanting pretend stuff and dreaming of what they don't have.

To avoid returning to Dickensian poverty, humanity needs a complete philosophical and design overhaul if we are to become as great as we keep telling ourselves we are. Modern architectural trends have a penchant for minimalist open plan spaces in a warped and vacuous attempt at balancing our aesthetic ideals to justifying ludicrous wealth by isolating objects of status. The white cube art gallery look of clean cut, man-made smooth angles whiting out all diversity of pigmentation with more space than one needs, displays vulnerability in reverse. The general idea is that less is more, which it hardly ever is in architecture. Minimalism tries to hide greed by presenting virginal white space in homologous importance to objects of opulence and projected beauty. In actuality, minimalism has proven to make people feel very uncomfortable. The solution is to re-evaluate, re-organise and re-build, living amongst trees, wildlife, green grass and near fresh water.

Picture a world where everything has organic shapes and ideas. You are connected to this deep knowledge and history. Your dreams are heard and feelings are met by nature's infinite aesthetics and forgiving inclination. Life is full of lush greens and reassuring browns. Water drips off leaves onto an absorbent, earthy ground as a colourful ladybird suns its wings. Your community are bathing in a lake close by, with others fishing out deep and splashing children's laughter. Words like *agenda* and *schedule* rarely surface as you are living without pretention, just being yourself. Happiness shimmers across the water in a meaningful moment of tranquillity. You never delay enjoyment these days. Nature and solid oak friendships are your guide to life. You didn't feel truly relaxed before in towns or cities, but now in nature you are home and it feels great. The best memories are made in nature.

In a super-huge community, little bubbles of staged personalities and airheaded domes of political correctness contaminate our individuality and goodness within. Humans have a competitive drive and hybrid of emotions which builds into a muddled collective consciousness, dissimilar in momentum and direction to our individual psyche. When a person is isolated for more than a few months they do strange repetitive things as their mind tries to come to terms with feelings of emptiness, panic, futility and despair by creating it's own narrative and voices. Now divorced from groupthink and the matrix, the lonely mind has an individual awakening which questions the sense of the outside paradigm with real objectivity and raw cynicism. These newfound thoughts have no social pull and can be uncontrollable as no-one ever teaches a person to be an individual.

Sometimes I think it would be lovely to be as free as a bird until I see about 50 seagulls fighting over a slice of bread.

Humanity has inventively fought hard enough to evolve into directors of our own destiny. We look, poke, probe, dissect and experiment on intricate creature's worlds without any fear of reprisal. People are like freak aliens on a planet observing wildlife either staying well away from us or barely eking out survival from our excessive rubbish tips.

Having cracked the big hunt for food problem, we're on unsteady ground to claim ignorance about destroying so much of our wildlife heritage. Humans are rapidly exhausting an unsustainable lifestyle and have the time, space and motive to change our fortunes. A bold move would not be a reckless gamble when a hollow future is in store. Humanity has simply outgrown the city model and needs to gradually vacate the premises before we're evicted by natural law.

Happiness

The birth of happiness.

Happiness is good fortune

You can't buy happiness but you can buy misery. In order to build a great society, most people need to feel reasonably happy most of the time. Therefore, happiness is the positive staple mindset we should all be cultivating, not a negative competitiveness with neighbours and acquaintances. A sure sign you're happy and content is you don't crave money. Always thinking about how you could use more money creates a disproportionate representation of people's true worth and is frequently used to dismiss bad behaviour instead of rewarding good deeds. Retail is far from long-term therapy. It's just a quick fix and a fool's trap. Consumerism makes everything seem mundane and takes the fun out of getting something special when you deserve it. When your heart shines with love and kindness you don't care what possessions other people have. Craving social status via wealth makes people mean-spirited and is a sign of ignorance. Be your own person, not one of the scared sheep who can't be trusted.

> Society has a bad habit of hurting decent people and rewarding the shits.

In this alphabetized society we can easily lose perspective of our emotions and character, as well as time. A vacuous society begins to believe that a mansion is more important than a child's well-being. If emotionally secure, children become self-supporting, content and capable human beings who go on to create a nest full of more nurtured happiness and also protect the elderly in return. At some stage of earnestness, to be happy we approach a fork in the road with a sign to the left saying, 'Be wealthy and worshipped,' or the right sign, 'Value emotions and decency.' Materialism leads us away from our natural sunshine source of happiness like cajoling salesmen forcing an unwanted insurance policy. The heavily promoted con that fame could turn your life from rags to riches in a week has harmfully infiltrated our fragile, easily corrupted psyches. By all means destroy yourself with monetary ambition, I just ask nicely you only do this without upsetting others.

> Above all else, materialism is the culprit bringing us to our knees.

It takes a good 5 years after being indoctrinated by our national educational systems to break one's mind free from the materialistic matrix, which is an essential requirement of achieving happiness. So how can we *not* go mental in a society which promotes, wants and is designed to make us digest lies? How do we metaphorically walk on hell's hot coals without getting burnt? Strangely, one of the first ways to become happy is to become comfortable with unhappiness. By accepting drudgery and your lot, you instantly reduce dissatisfaction levels which maximises your free time. Be grateful for what you have by living within your means. Constantly pushing our poser limits to impress people, plucks contentment out of her *happy-go-lucky* shell and skewers it like a winkle in a seagull's starving beak.

Bear in mind our survival aspirations are usually higher than our capabilities.

> Most people are very dull and disappointing but a few shine like a lodestar and renew your faith in humanity.

Experiencing the cycle of life in all its guises make us feel normal and cheery, and collects praise along the way. Tasty food, playing games, then finding a partner and having kids who have kids to play with you again as a doting grandparent. We always need to feel like integral members of work and family groups to prevent stagnation, a hole in our character résumé and the fear of isolation that so loves to taunt a sorrowful attitude. Our deceitful society is almost the sole cause of most people's unhappiness as it magnetises its pawns against their free will. Illnesses, depression and noise levels rise as testosterone and sperm counts lower to cope with a sardine packed society. A garden-shed and coffee-shop disenfranchised community which doesn't speak its mind, creates a lack of direction which ranks high on reasons for wandering into misery. To keep us further pinned down, false fears like terrorism or made-up dangerous viruses are banded about like they're part of our daily lives. The world is being taken over by James Bond type villains, the big problem being all of the double O's are on their side. The sheep are mainly afraid to hear medical and political truth because they can't bear to think how truly ruthless and evil their masters are. Lost sheep tend to wander into the path of wolves.

Happiness is not letting injustice get the better of you and allowing people to be stressed without losing energy. It's a difficult balance between exploring and facing the truth of the world as well as accepting that random bad things just happen and nasty people are usually victims themselves. Humans will be humans and a small sum of you are terribly nice people. On the whole, exclusively finding happiness vicariously is a big mistake.

Keep your spirits high, your bodies healthy, your friendships warm and your mind full of enthusiasm to send evil back to hell.

Living in a state of on-off anger, or feeling perpetual hatred towards this unfair system or conniving enemies is a sure-fire way to burn your integrity to the ground and make you bitterly unhappy. Forgiveness, non-judgmental thoughts and soulful music are weighty stepping stones towards happiness. With forgiveness in your heart you will not harbour the fear of repeated torment which invites more pain. It takes great mental strength to forgive whilst being mindful of your continued well-being. True forgiveness must be without reins like a seahorse, balanced and delicate. Let every last wave of forgiveness flood through you holding no current back. Forgiveness doesn't mean opening opportunities for wrongdoers to hurt you again, quite the contrary. It's about understanding their internal conflicts, stopping them from harming others and knowing how to end their misery too. If they don't seek forgiveness, don't forgive them unless for yourself, you need to psychologically move on. There's not much point forgiving someone who's not ready to be blessed as it won't help them and they may vex you again when your guard is down. The coward needs to feel your courage and so do you otherwise you'll play the victim and every victim has a villain.

The evil masterminds behind the covid scamdemic must never be forgotten or forgiven.

Beware the manipulative actor feigning false sorrow for their misdeeds and begging for forgiveness with a hammy performance. Some freaks pretend to relish unhappiness because they know no better and seek revenge for having a refrigerator mother. Harbouring any resentment towards oppressors can fester in you like worm rot, yet you don't want to be taken for a ride or make light of the previous harm caused. Absolute forgiveness can easily manifest into gullibility which strengthens iniquitous minds. Unconditional forgiveness frequently let's evil people off the hook which is no good for personal or social balance. If the wrongdoer gets off too lightly and isn't sorry they are likely to repeat the cycle of hatred. Before facing the golden gateway of forgiveness the bully should be made to see the light by feeling the harm they caused. A sincere wrongdoer will ask and do what is best for their victim.

Mother figurehead.

The family fortress

Good families are the nucleus of happiness. Is happiness a lost place (metaphysical), a mental position or decision (psychological), a born feeling (scientific), or a group democracy and consensus (collective consciousness)? It's *all* of the above and it starts at home.

Hopefully so, your home is the refuge where all woes can be sorted, emotional support gained and lifestyle reflected upon. The world may not agree with you but your home always does. These mostly orange and red brick nests with double-glazed views should be a sanctuary from nastiness. Society can be cruel to its human pets, yet the home is a stronghold of love, reinforced beliefs, entertainment and if happiness is at home, it's a heartfelt castle bonding those in its keep.

> Truth bomb: society started to fall apart when families did.

Family unity is the core of happiness. When everything falls apart *who you gonna call?* In fortunate people's cases it's the parents nearly every time, or grandparents, siblings, auntie's and uncles, cousins or friends. Good family and friends will pull you out of your shell and amplify your existing happiness. Without the nuclear family unit we'd readily get turned into slaves. Families are powerful units which oppose globalist's shuffling people around the world as economic commodities. The great qualities, attributes, laughs, memories and warm family bonds cradled by our single minds, transcend material pleasures. Happiness also comes from the pride we take in our family's good beliefs and all the good achievements your close relatives have made in your family's name.

I would follow you to the ends of the Earth
because there would never be
an end with you.

Good parenting is the heartbeat of human existence. An octopus mother often ends up ingesting her own arms for food to ensure her eggs stay constantly protected and oxygenised by water currents. Most human parents don't seem quite so committed these days. The rapid disintegration of the bonded family bloodline in modern times is a pivotal reason for alarming rises in mental illness and social anxiety. It's a statistical fact that broken families breed many more unhappy bunnies than stable families: biological dad to replacement step dad, to another emotional disruption, argument after another uncertainty and where does it all end; in misery, materialism and distraction from our main goals to work together for the greater good. When divorce became as effortless as getting a refund from Amazon, child sexual abuse rocketed in tandem. A splintered society grows less backbone than jellyfish.

Another truth bomb: feminism
tried to kill the family unit.

Children are usually the victims of immaturity, selfishness and mislaid fantasies. Everyone's lives count and everybody involved is affected. Thinking you've only got one life is a thought of desperation which leads to indecent decisions. Encouraging children to be mentally ill victims of society produces weak-minded adult scroungers. Ambiguity and indecisiveness create unhappiness and depression. Life expectations are simply too high and delusional in a contemporary, makeshift society where broken branches have fake ideas grafted on.

Our devilish leaders will always use a divide and conquer strategy to break families down into individuals to make it much easier to exploit people in an atmosphere of insecurity. The antidote is to banish transitory desires, to concentrate on reality and strengthen the roots of your family tree with nimble care and consideration. Detaching from your destiny by putting other people's happiness first is at the heart of you feeling happy.

One final truth bomb: promoting transgender in schools fucks children's minds up.

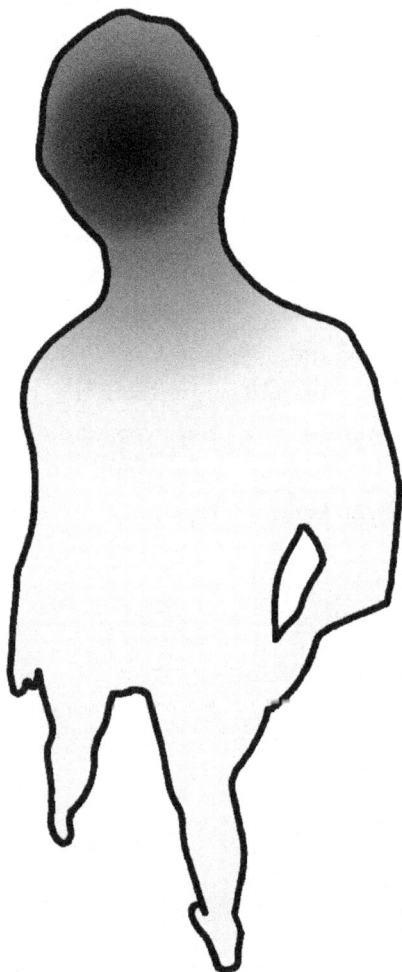

Choose your perspective.

Behaviour defines you

It's best to stick on the checkout you're already on. Many humans don't know how to enjoy life without the aid of someone else's money or performance effort. A *nanny state* makes people apathetic, unresourceful and some very lazy. Enjoyment has become too externalised. Socialising is not an achievement. Hobbies, indoors craft and creativity develop the brain to produce its own happy scenarios. Other people like to watch a good movie to make themselves happy, or perhaps walk the dog, or go somewhere brand new. We all have our individually nuanced strategies for reproducing happiness and each time we repeat our favourite type of event the plan either improves or becomes weirder in the search for the happiness formula and elixir of life.

If you want to be happy it's essential to find your tribe even if you like your own company most of the time. Just knowing like-minded people exist helps you relax and find balance.

In daily life we routinely pick our point of view. Being happy is a cultivated choice you make. Always angle yourself towards the light. Happiness is a state of *being* which rises to the surface of your consciousness when things are all going right and you are behaving well. Being happy stops you being sad. Happy feelings come naturally to us, yet struggle to plume in our complex and stressful society. So much so, the search for happiness in this most unnatural of settings can be warped to a point where sexual asphyxiation, child abuse, odd masturbatory habits, projected narcissism, voyeuristic misfortune and a whole host of other sick plays provide an inverted happiness to lots of lonely individuals. Conscience is surprisingly easy to bury for many years on end, but when you begin striving for happiness it keeps tripping-up your plans until you follow the rope back to where it all began, say sorry and mean it. Happiness is a time-traveller.

On average, a female orgasm is reached after about 10-20 minutes of sexual intercourse. Male ejaculation occurs after just 2-3 minutes, on average. Those numbers don't tally satisfyingly.

Of non perverse or moderate natures, many people are so void of understanding what happiness is and how to achieve it, they get stuck in a boring rut of doing the same originally happy task so many times over it makes them unhappy and disappointed in their lack of ability to look for happiness, which in itself causes more unhappiness. Others search so far they lose opportunities for bliss by giving too much of themselves to newcomers to seek constant thrills, or try so hard to find their core personality they lose the ability to find happiness in simplicity. Happiness is what is happy to you, not what everyone else says it is. Live for the moment, not what's promised around the corner. Being happy is a positive way of encouraging you through life's traumas and helps you to appreciate and become the good times. A life full of clouds doesn't matter if you are the sun.

Happiness is way too low down
on most people's agenda.

Dancing, sports and endorphin releasing exercise make many folk happy, or become less unhappy. Exercise is a good technique for bringing out happiness, but if you've been lethargic and/or sad for too long it can rapidly worsen your depression, causing further exhaustion and muscular stress if you don't stay within your body's limits, building up very slowly. Do most things when you feel like it and read your capabilities. Anything forced through an unfriendly schedule just exacerbates moodiness. Happiness knows what to do at the right time – flowing naturally where you're meant to be – allowing and affording time to exist happily. Let things happen when they want to happen.

It's obviously not possible to feel extreme joy all the time, yet by cultivating acceptance and smart mental engineering over an artificially moulded city, you can definitely stay constantly happy. With staunch resistance, the routine grind turns to determination: unhappy people get ignored; disappointments are approached with puissance; tiredness becomes calm; and noise and chaos one's inner peace. Happiness should be like a prevailing obelisk in your mind to be worshipped. Good chemistry, friends and great opportunities come and go, and happy thoughts connect them all. Happiness can erode any malcontent and relax the tightest of tensions, bringing a fluid consistency, an equilibrium and humanity into our complex technological arena. A state of bliss won't be achieved by gambling, exploiting others, excessive drinking, big lies, wanting more than reasonable and mainly trying to be who you're not. You must have a go at trying to make the world a better place for having you in it.

Happiness is different for everyone but the feeling of being happy unites us all.

Happiness is a rocking-chair within all of us which our minds need to practice swaying in. And one of the best places to ensure happiness is in the bed with good sex and sleep. If happiness was a hand-held link of friendship, then going to bed without any anxiety stirring inside in your head is a daisy chain of friends. Never go to bed with unresolved relationship arguments or fears otherwise the worry will break your deep sleep.

Clearing the air after a disagreement is vital to stop festering malcontents dragging your mind through morning ashes. If nighttime goes unchecked, whirling worries breed at an alarming pace like fire ants in your brain. No-one ever mentions sleep. A good bank of early nights prevents you from succumbing to most colds and flu. Good sleep almost equates happiness because a well rested mind can cope with almost anything. If you're sleep deprived, ill, obese, etc, your mind won't listen to much reason. It will just keep telling you you're not ready for action so be afraid or wary.

> Sometimes stargazing is all you need
> to brighten a dark mood.

Psychology has its limits, so we must do our best to prepare properly for the challenges that face us. Last minute psychological techniques to pull yourself out of trouble have minimal impact. Knowing who you are, where you're going and what you're capable of makes you totally up for life. The idea is to not get into a bad state in the first place. A good schedule and preparation will prevent having to resort to coping strategies. Be your own parent. Monitor yourself as if you were another person guarding your behaviour and pat yourself on the back for getting things right.

> The best counsel in the
> whole world is to go outside.

If you want to be happy, don't watch the news. Stay within your energy reserves. Walk with nature. Never act desperately or let anyone ever put you down. Strive to make your heaviest critics think twice on their harsh judgments for the sake of your own conscience. Boost your confidence all the time and project your voice more. Listen to your favourite music. Sing or whistle lots. Be full of love or find love. Learn how to cope with being rejected. Have plenty of chats, think of others first, play fairly and play loads.

Renounce narcissism and brand names in exchange for character and quality. Worship family moments. Stay calm as much as possible and offer your destiny to the universe. Just potter around for a few days doing odd jobs and woolgathering, sleep and socialise lots. Generally take everything less seriously. Don't get wound-up by ignorant neighbours or colleagues. The world is full of negative critics, so don't be your own.

Your journey is your end.

Control your own assumptions by letting people be themselves, meditate, resist being petty and make friends. And most importantly, remember to aim for happiness before all else. Contrary to what lots of people believe about genetics or fate, happiness is definitely a life skill which can be learnt by everyone. Happiness only bows to raw necessity. The feeling of happiness is warm through and through. You just know when you've arrived at mega-happiness station. That magnificent feeling is temporary and we're happy with that.

Unhappy people with money never understand how poor people can be happy.

Enjoy the ride.

A positive switch

Happiness is often located in the middle. Qualities like sensible negotiation, mature compromise and empathy encourage happy situations. Seeing the potential good in everyone is another path. Even corrupt, evil people were babies once. Understanding another person's downfall is a way of giving your happiness more nutrients. Don't waste your time going on about negative people, places or events in the past or present. Moaning drags you and everyone else down. If you must, get it over and done with and out of your system in a few sentences.

Some broken record minds living the victimhood dream really know how to milk every last drop of fake misery out. What's the point of living they may depressingly surmise on a bad day. What's the point of not living, we retort with logic and a passion for life. Being able to moan is a kind of privilege. Don't dwell on what's gone wrong or you'll foster a nocebo effect. Better to accept the world's failures, take the positive lessons learnt and get on with enjoying your life. Less talk and chewing the cud, more laughter and action instead. Negative assumptions are made by players who can't think more than one chess move ahead.

One thing is for sure, you're never going to win anything by taking no action and just moaning.

Every thought inside your mind must be positive and constructive as well as every word that comes out of your mouth. Don't let a repetitious, negative voice set you up for a fall. You can do anything you realistically set your positive mind to. Every hour is another hour you could be having fun. Lighten-up, enjoy your family and the fascinating variety in the world. Don't allow life to drag like it's a chore. You must make a conscious effort to enjoy things before your subconscious drifts into the well trodden negativity of no man's land. If you deliberately delay and procrastinate, events will move towards you anyway and you'll feel trapped.

To avoid getting stuck in a rut, change your tasks and environment every couple of hours if you can. Also, it's important try something new every week – no matter how small – to stay flexible and prevent fear setting in. It's not enough to just stave off bad feelings with temporary cures because they may creep back. You must wipe out the bad past and architect a new enjoyable future. The past cannot change, but your future is unwritten. Nothing is stopping you from filling that space with success. Once you have turned the corner into a world of happiness, keep walking. Success means handling your emotions and treating everybody with respect and the dignity all life forms deserve.

By detaching from your destiny
you're more likely to fulfil it.

You are what you create and become what environment you put yourself into. If you try and control the world you won't be able to control yourself in the end. Everyone should at least become a believer in themselves. You will make many mistakes on a road to recovery or betterment. The winners in life accept their mistakes and keep getting up after a fall. You may have taught yourself to wander, now teach yourself balance, stability and flexibility. Our minds exist and fluctuate in three main fields of thought: base survival, normal living and higher purpose. We start from psychological ground roots and work our way up to clear skies of happiness. *Thinking* is the only truly unfettered pastime with absolutely no constraints or conditions attached. A thought is as naked as the wind, as big as your brain's universe and as muddled or complete as you wish.

Ideas and opinions don't cost a penny so nothing is stopping you creating your own escape world inside your mind for free. Adopt self-hypnosis, positive auto-suggestion and visualisation techniques as a regular way of life. Let your subconscious soak up many motivational lines too, like; be positive because negativity is never a choice. Also, find people who inspire you to improve and appreciate living more. And let's not forget to try and see the funny side of everything. Laughter lifts your chemistry and spirits, giving you breathing space to do the right things and show the better side of yourself.

Always look on the bright side of things. As soon as something goes wrong, practice finding a little positive nugget hiding in the bundle of confused stress. Intelligence is measured by how well you perceive reality. Don't overreact to unwelcomed letters, people backbiting and small things in general. Be aloof if need be. Be confident in what you know is right. Take time to stop and look at things of interest. Let music into your life. The meaning of life is to leave the world a better place before you leave and to make each day better than the one before.

> I want my whole life to be a
> feel-good panda news story.

Gain perspective by espousing eternal values. Perceiving time as an everlasting concept is key to ridding yourself of unhappiness. Our biological mechanics build momentum of thought and string energies into character. Take a big step back and we wonder how anyone not facing a war or life threatening situation can possibly get themselves into such a terrific state about often not much. The mind is so powerful, yet uncontrollable, all of us struggle to comprehend, let alone harness its full potential. The fear of how ephemeral and out of control our minestrone soup-like emotions are, forces us to form a square mode of living, way less dynamic and inspirational than desired. Society looks to stabilize itself by taming the ferocious animal inside. Your mind is a wild horse that lets you have a ride now and again for its own sake and will unseat you if you challenge its organic authority.

> The key is to view everything
> with eternal light.

A crucial piece of happiness is pretending and then feeling you don't exist as a corporeal embodiment of political pressures, where an impermanent state of well-being cares not for your destiny. Controlling emotions tend to cram the mind up. Your heart can easily tell you what *is* and what is *not* yours by right. Once we see and believe ourselves as irrelevant without losing confidence, then happiness develops into universal balance. The path to happiness and enlightenment only begins by calmly and unconcernedly watching the world go by, avoiding unhappy pockets of malcontent.

What makes you happy these days?
Most people say family, laughter
and their dog in that order.

To further attain a blissful mind responsible for its condition we must extend this good energy into our community like travelling seeds in the air and confront, deal with and transform to the best of our abilities all negative obstacles. You choosing to stand in the way of tyranny is symbolic of finding the extra energy happiness supplies and of seeking the truth needed to be at one with yourself. Being enlightened is simply feeling happy for longer than normal on a regular basis. Our brains are veined to seek out happiness as roots water. Happiness comes in as many ways as we can imagine, but all varieties of people on this planet find happiness from the same sources of truth, unique achievement, generosity of spirit, sunlight and love – all co-existing in a natural landscape.

Society

The daily grind.

The devil is in the detail

Fighting back is as important as forgiveness. When winter is here, many people wish for Spring and then Summer instead of enjoying any snow and fireside cuddles in the moment. Nature goes at its own pace and we'd do well to gel with it instead of always wishing for different weather. Humans are a frightfully impatient species and nature's elements were supposed to slow us down, but we won, we actually temporarily defeated nature and now await the inevitable payback.

Agriculture conquered the daily food hunting crisis, yet humanity has bizarrely managed to turn a fight for survival into a fight between ourselves for even more luxurious comfort, leaving billions of people back at square one poverty. Humans should be really enjoying their evolutionary luck and doing whatever they fancy after a few daily light tasks to keep the social wheel turning. Instead, most of us are rushing around like blue-arsed flies getting all stressed-up about stuff to feed the dragons. What madness has befallen us weird human beings who nowadays are often seen wearing masks while driving on their own and even when swimming for no logical reason. Our incessant ladder climb for status worked in the jungle, but is an unmitigated disaster in a boomtown society. Searching for glorification and adulation has upset the group power dynamic, giving megalomaniacs carte blanche to take charge using money as the ultimate weapon of subjugation. The accumulation of money is the devil in full swing. Social trouble arises when we don't know who we are and how to see the truth in others. Fighting against the heavy currents in a goldfish bowl society, we forget to look through the glass to see who's swirling the water.

To everyone's stunned disbelief, a relatively small cult of hellish psychos have taken over the world and plan to send everyone but them to heaven.

In real life we have virtually no human rights, politics is a circus and freedom of speech is as dead as a dodo. Emergency decrees are the skeleton key to dictatorships. Unless we get the chance for an uncorrupted vote on how the system works or how tax money is spent, we have no democracy. Advertisement, political correctness, fashion, modern art, fake history and media hype are just a few of the thousands of disseminating policies and sly apparatuses leaders apply to disband free thinking and lifestyle choices. We are fed more misinformation and have more groups and sects than transgender operations in full swing. Soon we'll reach a point in society where most people won't know what they are. Divisive politics has overtaken science: men can't breastfeed and if everyone was gay, without test tube babies, the human race would die out. Think of the thousands of dedicated female athletes who spend years putting their heart and soul into their passion and developing skills, soon to be gradually taken over by female trans athletes who still have the strength of men. Unfair and twisted is an understatement. Society became a laughing stock when the two genders from X and Y chromosomes mutated into a multifarious language with its own alphabet. Next, the gender letters will demand their own supermarket food aisle. By tolerating everything without question on some misguided belief that makes you look like an educated and nice person, you'll end up the fool who helps a burglar steal your possessions. Omnisexuality and multiculturalism dilutes all cultures until you look to abandon your own. Government ringleaders will turn your beliefs upside-down until you end up balancing on your head unless you stand strong. Too many people nowadays have no self-belief. Hordes of well-meaning people have gone round the fucking bend trying to appease bizarre social norms and are so divorced from their natural survival instincts it's like they're floating on candyfloss cloud nine.

The irony is the woke culture are fast asleep.

You can't say this and you can't say that in moron city where real opinions are deemed gauche. The devilish idea is to manufacture so many social contradictions no-one knows where they stand or what they believe in anymore. Continuous distractions rooted from blatant government lies infiltrate your mind and cause internal conflict. They get you looking into every last insignificant detail of stuff that doesn't remotely matter so you don't see the truth. By chasing their tails for tittle-tattle, the masses fail to notice the puppet masters don't even give the dog a bone. Calculatingly giving minority groups beneficial treatment over patriots of their land, pulls the rug from under social stability, making people feel insignificant and unappreciated. A joker society which makes a mockery out of nature's design will collapse like the proverbial house of cards. Nature is a magnificent binding force in our lives we don't access enough. The matrix has a nasty habit of making you forget how healing the great outdoors is.

The break from nature divided our species into thousands of disunited tribes, all desperately trying to recreate small communities within the jumbled swarms of metropolis mayhem. Dispersed societies have scattered our minds into a continuous search for identity which has unfortunately been easily exploited by wannabe kaisers who promote further divide and conquer agendas to deliberately undermine moral and religious foundations. Perversely, the heinously larger a society becomes, the less the populous have control over their leaders. It has often been said that only a few handfuls of powerful tycoons orchestrate the entire world's paradigm, playing God whilst acting like Satan. Evil is rarely born. By and large, people become the position they inherit. We are opportunists designed to take advantage of fortuitous circumstances. It's upsetting to think how many people would commit horrid crimes if they knew they could get away with it. Everyone is comprised of both good and evil. We are a suicidal race striding into the abyss like the Four Horsemen of the Apocalypse.

In modern times, the basic reason why evil keeps rising to the top is because too many good people are comfortable at the bottom.

It's a commonly held myth that the obscenely wealthy classes keep societies financially afloat, whereas in reality the workers pay for themselves many times over. We the people, keep the upper crust in luxury and they reward us by stealing our hard earned money and imprinting, imposing, bullying and drumming lies into our work-tired brains until the cows come home.

The NWO have contempt for us and the feeling is mutual. Without us they're finished because we operate and know everything, so their task is to keep us hemmed in, distracted and entertained or face the wrath of the mob. If humans *really* want to change this caustic social archetype, the average person needs to become more resourceful, independent, forceful, proud and believe in their worth. To free ourselves from economic thralldom, our first gargantuan problem is overthrowing these super wealthy dynasties and oligarchs dominating us plebeians since they stole all common land from the people many centuries ago.

We can't lounge around and wait until their natural reign to end with the collapse of materialism because they will simply create a new fake financial system and make hay by owning all the properties. And we won't be able to kindly persuade them to stop being pointless exploiters of people and dragon hoarders of wealth either because they are deeply disturbed, psychopathic individuals who thrive on the twisted spoils of corruption and making normal people miserable. Many globalist moguls have been linked to worldwide paedophile rings and missing children cases, some involving monstrous satanic sacrifices. Their minds are cold, lizard-like, scaly isolations with no higher purpose.

These are not creatures anyone can reason with over a cup of Darjeeling without a show of fierceness. Most of the world's wealthiest billionaires have crossed moral lines of no return. Hoisted by their own petard they spend every day pretending they are someone they're not, exacerbating their twisted and duplicitous thoughts. The insane and tyrannical mind wants to tame the uncontrollable, so it's no surprise the cult billionaires' aim is to control the world's climate.

Anyone who makes plans to dim the sun's light is a fruitcake at best.

The uber rich were usually once unloved children and now can't trust anyone so all they can think of doing is ruining everyone else's happiness in an infantile, jealous type of revenge. That's the paltry sum of their real worth. They had their childhoods stolen from them, therefore many end up child molesters with sick, infanticide minds. The monetary system gives them a focus away from their internal torment. These soulless creatures feel safe manipulating figures and global markets, which then gives them the idea of manipulating people. They are weak people who have never come to terms with being unloved by their parents so feel very separate and isolated from the rest of the world, often struggling to form normal relationships, exhibiting perversions and unnatural quirks which all lead to a super ego replacing the mother, choosing rape and murder over crying and healing.

All the NWO leaders and their political puppets have noticeably dark, demonic and soul-sucking looking eyes making you wonder if they're a different species taking over. These heartless, sadistic things not only lack any compassion and kindness, they spread death everywhere they go. They are insanely wealthy oddities, masquerading as geniuses, couldn't give away their entire fortune to save their own lives if they had to which shows how little psychological power they really have - locked into a miserable trap of sycophantic aggrandisement and insanely addicted to the drug of greed which is powered by negative energies. They too, just like the sheep, are petrified of death, throwing billions of dollars into organ replacement technology, bio-robotics, stem cell research, etc, in a vain and pointless attempt to achieve immortality.

Deep down inside, every maniac billionaire just wants a normal life full of family love without the headaches and stress that excessive wealth attracts. Many of us dream of having their money, yet their subconscious dreams about being you. Such is the widespread inability of modern citizens to be happy with the small patch of grass they have. The grass is only greener if you're stuck in a field ploughed full of manure.

If you're not doing your little bit to raise awareness you're accepting of tyranny.

Underestimate the greatness of nice people at our own peril. Positive evolutionary change will only happen if the timid sheep learn how to tame the wealthy weaklings impersonating wolves. And we will only beat these globalist moguls by all being united behind the common goal of fairness. Global kindness and civil disobedience are two great starting points to save us all from tyranny. And kindness does not mean weakness, it means helping people in need with your courageous heart. Few people are brave anarchists or principled heroes though. Most of us just want to get by as easily as possible and believe that life is for living not leading. But by acting like spineless mysophobes (people scared of germs) in a city of manic competing animals, the workers are literally asking to be dictated to. The plan is to give you an end of world feeling so you submit to the Grim Reaper but you won't submit, you won't ever stop fighting tyranny, you won't accept slavery and genocide as the new normal, you'll never give up or have anyone talk to you like a second-class citizen because you are right.

Bullying is a way of stealing
souls to cure loneliness.

Freedom was never gained without a global punch-up. Nowadays, the gigantic world population makes defeating dictators way more doable than in the past, thus their maniac depopulation plans. We can only blame ourselves for wanting to know our position rather than standing in our rightful place and being prepared to die defending it. Let's have some foresight and act before poverty and starvation force our hands to action.

Alien spacecraft.

Origins of the matrix

Aren't we just animals afraid of loud noises and the dark?
If you're feeling rebellious, mischievous or just plain bored at a dinner party and want to kick-start a damn good argument, just start discussing The Bible versus Charles Darwin's book On the Origin of Species and you're guaranteed uproar with no repeat invite. Chuck in some cheeky chats about war, flat-earther theories and anti-feminism and you'll be banned from cocktail parties for life.

The origin of human existence treads upon the most personal and delicate aspects of people's profound beliefs and emotional knowledge which sets their rhythm for life and peace of mind. Humans find anyone challenging their beliefs enormously stressful so they get defensive, ugly and even violent at times when someone shatters their reality. Just calmly talking about someone's precious philosophy and practical guide to life can end in tears because few people are big enough to let reason and probability change their mind about hallowed, private subjects.

The covid plandemic touches plenty of raw nerves too, showing you how most people are not able to discuss their strongly held beliefs with the opposition without throwing a temper tantrum or displaying anger. The God versus Evolution debate stirs up about five times that level of antipathy, so it's hard to stay focussed, rational and come to the right conclusions when personal beliefs and family persuasion cloud judgments. A heated religious debate ironically becomes survival of the fittest.

Cherish people who allow their beliefs to be challenged, for they are open-minded and probably right.

Hardly anyone is wise and mature enough to begin a discussion with a totally open mind, a clean philosophical slate, believing they could be wrong from the get-go. If you get upset when people question your beliefs you could simply be wrong. We have to accept the harsh reality that humans will believe absolutely any falsehood if it makes them feel better and provides hope, which doesn't bode well for our future.

Lying to ourselves for psychological comfort is as large a weakness as greed. You can virtually guarantee we all believe some lies and shy away from many truths to give us peace of mind. And if you don't regularly question and test your beliefs and principles you don't *know* if they're true. Most people confuse belief with proven facts and many established proofs are overturned by brand new discoveries.

The truth is only found after eliminating the gossip, propaganda, money, emotional ties and lies. We could all be completely and utterly wrong with our theories and if so there's no problem learning something new by widening the debate to invite better knowledge. What we need to do is look objectively at the evidence available – step by step –

with an open and detached mindset. Without truth we are often left with popular beliefs based on random feelings, not facts.

If you think man landed on the moon you're part of the problem and if you know Harry Potter was plagiarised you're part of the solution.

So many questions, so many guesses, yet so few good answers - if any. Was the world created in 7 days? Highly unlikely isn't it. Did the universe start from the Big Bang? Much less laughable, but something doesn't quite ring true about that explanation either. Is the Bible fact or fiction? Doesn't most fiction originate from some facts. Are we descendents of fish like the Coelacanth? Maybe Aquaman is.

Have aliens visited and changed the course of human history? Can we trust any leaked air force reports about UFO's or Roswell because we know governments like to spin wild conspiracy theories around planted conspiracies to disguise the truth. Have we evolved from a common primate ancestor? Some evidence suggests we have but nothing is written in stone, apart from fossils that is. Is there a divine creator, the one true God who began all of life? No-one can categorically prove so, yet we are constantly told there are clear signs of intelligent design and millions of people's intuition answers yes to that rooted question. If God created humans who created aliens? And if there is a divine creator, who created him?

Did giant humans the height of houses walk the Earth or is that complete bullshit to create controversy? Lots of faked photos, but the primate *Gigantopithecus blacki* could stand up to 10 feet tall and may have been the closest relative to Sasquatches. How did ancient humans create sophisticated mechanisms with cogs or build with perfectly carved blocks of rock weighing from 20 tons to over 1,100 tons. Maybe they broke the stone down into liquid using fire and/or natural chemicals, then poured it into the gaps of large blocks? Perhaps very little or absolutely nothing we have been taught or believe is real. To find the truth we must entertain extreme ignorance as a likely possibility and clear our impressionable minds of preconceived doctrines.

You can't ever back down from
the truth once it has enlightened you.

Most people have made their minds up what they believe about the origin of Man because we hate indecision and need to see a bigger picture, but the jury is still out as this never-ending metaphysical investigation continues. The problem with humans is our furtive imaginations happily fill in unknown gaps and invent whole subjects and beliefs that don't exist because we need hope, acceptance and to finalize our thoughts way before the raw truth makes an uncomfortable appearance. To repeat, deluding and deceiving ourselves is a common part of reaching closure and moving forward. We have no sensible way of measuring or validating feelings and personal experiences, so logical guesswork is what's left on the table.

Whatever your beliefs - each to their own - it's highly unlikely our violent species will survive long enough to know the absolute truth of our origins. For now, let's objectively look at the main sides of this debate and reach rational conclusions in a humble attempt to add knowledge, rather than defend pre-existing assumptions and moulded emotions. Everyone should be a lot more respectful of other people's beliefs if they're doing you no harm, instead of calling strangers a fool or an idiot just because they don't agree. Clear your mind and let us begin.

THEORIES OF EVOLUTION

Aggression and inventiveness has taken humans to the top of the evolutionary tree but not the canopy of our cognitive potential. Much human behaviour and decision making stems from our common chimpanzee kin, yet chimp genetic similarities with humans are likely much lower than most sources commonly claim at roughly 98%. Skipping the details, there's likely to be approximately an 85% similarity which explains why we can't reproduce with chimps or use their organs for transplants (much contemporary research regarding DNA sequencing and carbon dating is flawed, and sometimes wildly inaccurate). There does seem to be a weird conspiracy to mislead the populace into believing chimps have virtually identical genes to humans, leading many people to incorrectly think we evolved from chimps rather than sharing primate similarities. Similarly, lots of religious people are so busy telling atheists they don't understand the divine power of God, they fail to understand even the simple basics of Darwin's theories of evolution, misunderstanding humans to have popped into existence out of nowhere somewhere along the evolutionary timeline. In a similar vein, George Lemaître's 1927 Big Bang theory does not mean something from nothing. Regardless, the lack of knowledge and facts about our potential common ancestors leaves a big hole in proving Darwin's theories.

Since March 2020, *Homo sapiens* have proven to be sheep-like saps. Luckily, a new primate genus emerged called *Homo giwar* from Latin and Old Saxon meaning the earthly one who is aware. Jk.

Nevertheless, it's hard to dismiss the striking behavioural similarities primates have with humans. Maybe somewhere along the evolutionary tree, humans branched off to become a naked looking primate with much thinner and sparser hairs than his cousins, perhaps to help humans run longer distances by sweating more, helping the cooling down process. Chimps get all the press, but it seems likely that bonobos who look like smaller and thinner chimpanzees are more related to humans than chimps. These two species of the genus *Pan* were most likely separated by the formation of the Congo River about 1.5-2 million years ago and learning about their behaviour gives you a great insight into why you behave certain ways.

Bonobos operate a much more matriarchal troop than chimpanzees, are much less aggressive in captivity and they walk upright more. They stand as tall as chimps and are only slightly smaller. Like chimps they live in a fission-fusion society and all come back together at night to sleep in trees. Bonobos are famed for being peaceful primates in captivity, but field observations in the wild show they can be as aggressive as chimps and can also have alpha males as leaders. Most commonly though, female bonobos run the show and, like humans, they prefer to hangout and/or have sex with males who are even-tempered and pay them respect. Bonobo females who spend more time in heat than female chimpanzees, who frequently use copulation as a peacemaking strategy, are very sexually active and often practice homosexual behaviours. They are caring and look after their children until adulthood. Most interestingly the mother helps their male offspring find a suitable partner to mate with and can also defend him against other males. Bonobo troops do some wife swapping and copulations are both heterosexual and homosexual, sharing sex across group members and from all age ranges. Having greater freedom with who they have sex with than female chimps, just like humans the female bonobos choose to mate with the highest ranked males. Interestingly, bonobos are also the only animal apart from humans to be seen French kissing. Bonobos are more skilled at solving mental tasks than chimps, but their chimp neighbours are better at using tools.

A chimpanzee community chooses an alpha male to dominate largely female consensus. The alpha leader usually has a higher level of emotional intelligence than the other males and sometimes uses psychological manipulation to get what he wants by deliberately upsetting the tribe, exerting his physical prowess. Female chimps use tools more efficiently than male chimps which eventually evens-out the playing field in a multitude of ways. Alpha hierarchy is usually bloodline and unlike bonobos, chimps are highly territorial and not afraid of bloodshed. In bonobo, chimpanzee and human groups, females play a much larger role in decision making and have more influence than often acknowledged.

Bonobos are more emotional and nervous than chimpanzees, and can make informed risk assessments making them less likely to take chances (Stanford, John, Anton, 2012). Research by anthropologist James Rilling and company (2011) shows bonobos are also much more empathetic than chimps due to differences in the limbic system (a set of brain structures involved in many motivations and emotions, especially those related to fear and anger). Bonobos dislike violence. Their spontaneous efforts to appease aggression with sexual offers is very similar to how sheeple respond to stressful situations. What some people are willing to do to get out of a scrape is nothing short of animalistic.

Humans are so similar to chimps and bonobos, yet paradoxically so completely different it's baffling. We ape their behaviour impeccably but also sense fundamental differences which separate our minds from theirs. As we multiply and advance across the world, they are driven to extinction by us which is a cruel twist of fate. Perhaps all of the monkeys, apes and chimps de-evolved from humans due to poor diet. We always assume creatures improve, but some might very, very slowly die out and go backwards – albeit unlikely so. And with regards to the first primate mammals, proto-primates, there doesn't seem to be a morsel of convincing evidence linking common primate ancestors to humans.

Digging down into our basic drives, humans don't appear to be much different from chimps and bonobos. Driven by the primate desire to have sex with as many partners nature allows, human males become visceral victims of a monetary system which erroneously assesses a man's core value based on coin, often surmounting heart, brain and arm muscles. And females too enter into a now confused primitive gathering mode to sweep up as much materialistic safety as possible. In super-huge societies all of these base primordial patterns become anomalous games – losing the meaning and good intentions of evolutionary development. If we are to survive our own progressive strengths turned many weaknesses in a modern setting, humans have to counter-intuitively stop what we sometimes do best.

Just like chimpanzees, we are uncomfortable waiting in line for food when hungry and feel awkward hanging around waiting for an investment to materialise years later. Chimps grab what they can, when they can and gorge. We want immediate gains all the time, being short-term savers, thus short-term thinkers and decision makers which shall likely be our undoing. We are now caged and no longer wild, yet our genes still fight to return to an anachronistic order which isn't feasible or necessary nowadays and this causes people stress.

Can you trust in your beliefs if
you don't believe in yourself?

Charles Darwin's study of finches on different Galapagos islands showed us the birds evolved slightly differently to suit their varied environments. Thousands of generations of small behavioural and adaptive changes slowly altered the creatures to survive more successfully. For example, hominids gradually developed curves in their lower spine, more forward facing hips and longer legs to walk more efficiently to carry more food, forage and hunt better. Darwin's central natural selection idea is about successful adaptations being inherited to advance a species. Turtles, lizards, chimps, monkeys, etc, are still in our time whilst we have continued to advance much faster because they simply didn't need to adapt, is the theory. The large semi-aquatic reptiles (crocodiles, alligators and caiman) are perfect hunters and most importantly thrive where most humans don't, so there's no need for biological change. The most successful species' have always been small creatures and insects who can survive on next to nothing, many which haven't altered a great deal in hundreds of millions of years.

Erasmus Darwin, a doctor and Freemason, was Charles' grandfather whose ideas on human evolution no doubt sowed many seeds in his grandson's initiated mind. Charles Darwin's theories seem to add up when looking at a couple of pieces of the origin puzzle, but connect all the possible adaptations and unknowns into a complete historical picture and we have a one-dimensional, linear view which works out using convenient imagination but not on paper. Striking primate similarities with humans are betrayed by surges in evolution beyond the generational opportunities available in time to mutate so successfully. To jump from one species to another, even over millions of years, requires a series of mega-long-shots and some hops and skips across a vastly unexplored and unknown evolutionary timeline. We could very well have not climbed down from trees at all.

> Thinking, knowing, believing and proving are four totally different things.

Basically put and missing a few steps: originally grown from deoxyribonucleic acid (DNA); protocells, then bacteria to a slug-like organism (*Kimberella*, existing 535 myo); to an early vertebrate (*Haikouichthys*); then the earliest known articulated bony fish (*Guiyu oneiros*, ghost dream fish); tetrapods (four limbed animals); fishapods crawling out of the water (*Tiktaalik*); amniotes; synapsids; the earliest known mammaliamorph (*Adelobasileus*); the evolution of placenta; haplorhini (dry-nosed primates); to maybe an early hominid (*Proconsul*); and eventually developing into *Homo sapiens* is one school of thought. And the Sonic Hedgehog molecule holds the DNA recipe for limb development.

The Greek philosopher Anaximander (610-546 BC), perhaps the first philosopher to write down his work and the first to conceive a model of Earth floating without support, also first proposed that humans came from other animals, suggesting most likely fish because of foetal similarities. If we were going by teeth alone, the pacu and sheepshead fish teeth are very weirdly humanlike. Evolutionists says that dolphins breastfeed and breathe air from a blowhole after evolving over about 50 million years ago from a land mammal called *Pakicetus* who looked sort of like a wolf. Dolphins are to tuna fish as humans are to monkeys. We know cave people painted fish and human hybrids, and possibly aliens and their spacecraft too (one flying saucer drawing was found in the Niaux French caves, dating roughly between 13-10,000 BC, if we trust what archaeologists say).

Ancient Greek natural philosophers Empedocles and Lucretius also developed ideas on natural selection over a couple of thousand years before Charles Darwin, so Darwin's theories weren't remotely original: just another case of who you know and what the world powers want the world to believe so as to dismember the biggest opposition to their tyranny, the family unit. Darkness comes when people turn a blind eye to the light.

It's much better to be an open-minded conspiracy realist than a fucking idiot with eyes wide shut.

Going on contemporary information, there are a number of black and white hypotheses we could reach:

1. Planet Earth is billions of years older than scientists calculate and all creatures slowly evolved from bacteria, then fish, etc. Relatively unexplained sudden appearances in evolutionary terms occurred because those species had previously evolved.

2. Our species' observed adaptations are so small and negligible, more responses to the environment than adaptations and mutations, humans have been roughly the same since day dot. Therefore, either a scientific or divine creator, or gods made us. And perhaps God created life and then left never to return.

3. An alien species put us here from another milky way or universe, or other humans travelled here and colonized, or perhaps crashing meteorites carrying nucleobases kick-started human life.

4. A strange mixture of all or some of the aforementioned points, where a divine creator propagated an existing planet as well as possibly extraterrestrials disrupting the timeline.

5. It's beyond our comprehension to appreciate who we actually are. That is to say we can only partially interpret reality and our energy - totally misreading our animal or children of God status.

6. Time does not exist and we operate in multiple parallel universes which overlap continuously, confusing the concept of a timeline and swapping life over.

The whole mind-blowing conundrum lies in what happened at the very beginning, if a beginning at all. Was it evolutionary, divine enhancement or a direct species placement be it godly or alien?

In conclusion, there doesn't seem to be a distinct coevolution between primates and humans. Whilst acknowledging species adaptation is caused by a *need* to change, despite living in roughly the same jungle environment with only lessening food supplies and territory due to hunting and deforestation, it's still very unusual how other primates and creatures haven't evolved at all whilst we have apparently descended with untold modifications. That's because we haven't developed a great deal. Not only were humans roughly the same 300,000 years ago but the entire historical and archaeological timeline is completely wrong and it's much more likely humans have been around in our original form for tens, maybe hundreds of millions of years.

Undoubtedly, being successful predators we've created and annihilated many lost civilisations along the way during thriving warmer periods. We've literally reinvented the wheel many times over – entire empires cracking and sinking into oceans. History is a repeating cycle of bursting carbon dioxide life in between numerous major glaciations and significant ice ages: 5 of which may be the Huronian (2.4-2.1 billion years ago); Cryogenian (850-635 million years ago); Andean-Saharan (460-430 Ma); Karoo (360-260 Ma); and Quaternary glaciation (2.6 Ma to present). In brief, evolutionary theories feel like ideas put into our minds to detract us from reality, but many good lies have elements of truth to them.

Taking a shot in the dark to answer the seemingly impossible question of where humans came from – using intuitive guesswork to bridge ginormous gaps in discernable evolutionary and god knowledge – I'd guess that humans did not evolve from the sea and have never jumped species. There are thousands of anthropoidal similarities, traits and shared suites between many species and it doesn't mean we ever crossed evolutionary paths in nested hierarchies. Either an almighty energy built all the animals on Earth itself like in a wildlife park or maybe omnipotent powers too vast for our brains to understand somehow managed to transport/teleport all life onto this watery planet. Either way it's hard to prove because of the lack of intervention from our possible maker/makers - leaving us to fight it out alone.

Humanity badly needs a great awakening and now is the perfect time to fulfil our destiny by evolving harmony with nature after vanquishing evil from the land.

Humans are blindly heading towards WWIII which may be the final battle mentioned in the Bible's Book of Revelation, therefore surely if God is watching over his flock He will save the innocent and punish all evildoers. Time will tell. Truth will out. Humans are a continuous story of amazing potential wasted because they don't punish evil people enough. With regards to our origins, we cannot ignore many passages in Revelations becoming frighteningly true right now,

"...I know you have little strength, yet you have kept my word and have not denied my name. I will make those who are of the synagogue of Satan, who claim they are Jews though they are not, but are liars - I will make them come and fall down at your feet and acknowledge that I have loved you." (3:8-9)

"The rest of mankind that were not killed by these plagues still did not repent of the work of their hands; they did not stop worshipping demons, and idols of gold, silver, bronze, stone and wood - idols that cannot see hear or walk. Nor did they repent of their murders, their magic arts, their sexual immorality or their thefts." (9:20-21)

"Because of the signs he was given power to do on behalf of the first beast, he deceived the inhabitants of the earth. ...and cause all who refused to worship the image to be killed. He also forced everyone, small and great, rich and poor, free and slave, to receive a mark on his right hand or on his forehead, so that no-one could buy or sell unless he had the mark., which is the mark of the beast or the number of his name." (13:14-17)

"The first angel went and poured out his bowl on the land, and ugly and painful sores broke out on the people who had the mark of the beast and worshipped his image." (16:2)

"...It is done. I am the Alpha and the Omega, the Beginning and the End. To him who is thirsty I will give to

drink without cost from the spring of the water of life."
(21:6)

Parts of the Christian Bible can be incredibly prophetic to the
point of unquestioned contemporary reality. One could
readily draw uncanny and strong comparisons between the
mark of the beast and covid vaccines, and covid passports. In
some parts of the world the unvaccinated are restricted from
buying products and food like Revelations says (on previous
page). Others are imprisoned (2:10) for questioning the false
prophet (19:20) who deceived the nations (20:3), who
practices magic arts and falsehood (22:15), and deluded those
who received the mark. Certainly thousands of people are
now deeply regretting their decision to get the jab and feel
they were not properly informed of the ingredients and
potential harmful and deadly side-effects.

Furthermore, you could interpret people who are afraid of
covid as the cowardly that Revelations places in the fiery
lake of burning sulphur (21:8) because they worship
falsehood above truth and blame others for their irrational
fear. If there was a deadly disease going around there would
be no need to convince people to get the antidote. All evil
people have to do is plant seeds of doubt about your well-
being and weak minds will do the hard work for them.
Imagine finding out that what you thought would save you
from a deadly plague was the actual thing killing everyone.

Covid isn't airborne, waterborne or dangerously stubborn, it's
all born from evil lies. The covid lie has divided everyone in
the world even more than religion ever has. Viruses seem
more powerful than gods. It makes you wonder how many

other pandemics and national states of emergency were also faked to create dictatorships.

Alternatively and wildly speculating, perhaps the whole God concept, belief and/or reality is our naive projection and guesswork going along the right lines towards the truth, yet instead of a King of Kings in the form we have interpreted and written many stories on, a highly advanced outsider species could have discovered our fertile planet and kick-started life here for unknown purposes. Or maybe aliens just left after interfering in life here when they got or didn't get what they wanted which disrupted the balance like a foreign species eradicating indigenous species'. If there was a divine creator of all of life with such unimaginable power then surely He would not allow extraterrestrial forces to interfere with his divine creation, or perhaps aliens are fallen angels?

Some old and ancient paintings and tapestries display a number of unexplained images which could be interpreted as religious symbolism, but seem much more like alien depictions. In the background of a 15th century painting called The Madonna with Saint Giovannino, a man walking his dog looks up at the sky to what looks awfully like a UFO. Other notable alien spacecraft paintings or technology of real interest include: a flying disc firing a laser or light beam in The Annunciation with Saint Emidius (1486); a flying saucer with 4 beams of light in The Baptism of Christ (1710); a very high-tech looking sphere in the Glorification of the Eucharist (1600); a couple of weird looking spaceships in The Crucifixion Of Christ, Kosovan wall mural (1350); a clichéd flying saucer in the life of

Virgin Mary tapestry, (1330); the Valcamonica spacemen cave drawings in Italy (circa 10,000 BC); jellyfish looking spacecraft in the Svetishoveil Cathedral fresco The Crucifixion of Christ (1600's); the lunar module looking craft with landing legs rock art painted in Charama, India (circa 10,000 BC); and a handful of familiar hat shaped UFO's in the background of the Triumph of Summer, a Belgium tapestry (1538).

Even in the Bible, Ezekiel's vision of the Merkabah chariot, that looked awesome like glowing metal, sparkling like chrysoberyl and ice, speeding back and forth like flashes of lightning, flown by creatures with human form, could easily be interpreted as an alien spaceship. In material terms one could readily argue there's more circumstantial evidence that aliens exist than God does. However, aliens not revealing themselves to humanity feels as illogical as astronauts never returning to the moon since 1972, but perhaps they understandably don't want to be shot down by fighter jets or attacked knowing what violent, fearful creatures we are. Aliens have every reason to be cautious of humans because every military force in the world would love to get their hands on super advanced technology.

There are many good reasons why ET might want to reject direct contact with humans. Our rudimentary weapons would probably still badly damage their ships and kill individual aliens walking among us. Why take risks you don't need to. Or maybe planet Earth is an intergalactic zoo for aliens to visit on a nice day out to see what their ancestors created. Do you bother talking to less intelligent cattle like sheep and cows you watch in fields. Perhaps aliens may have a totally unimaginable reason for coming here to tap resources, do science experiments, etc, and have absolutely no interest in humans whatsoever. We could be like pesky flies annoying them as they go about their business. Alternatively, their intentions may be sinister, therefore it makes sense to hide from the species you are covertly hurting and experimenting on.

Lots of out-of-place artefacts, writings and cultural beliefs throw mystery over the origins of humankind conundrum, such as the Dogon Myth where the Dogon tribe (about 100,000 members occupying a region in Mali, West Africa in the Homburi mountains near Timbuktu) speak of the Nommos who visited Earth on a large spaceship a number of times from a companion star to Sirius (the brightest star in Earth's night sky, also known as the Dog Star, 8.6 light-years from our planet and moving on a direct course towards our solar system). The Dogon people are possibly from Egyptian decent and their astronomical legends go back over 5,000 years.

To a healthy cynic, on first impressions it all sounds like possible superstitious poppycock until you find out that French anthropologists Dr Marcel Griaule and Dr Germaine Dieterlen came across a number of ancient artefacts (one at least 400 years old) from Dogon elders describing the white dwarf star Sirius B (they named Po Tolo), which was only determined to exist by Western scientists in the 1920's because of its gravitational influence on Sirius A's movements. Furthermore, Sirius B was not photographed until 1970 or seen through a telescope until 1862 by American astronomer A.G. Clark, thousands of years after the Dogon people apparently mentioned it. On further investigation, the Dogon's who claimed that amphibious looking extraterrestrial beings have spoken to them describing the Sirius star system, knew previously unknown details about our solar system, possibly predicting that Po Tolo's orbit around Sirius was 50 years (50.04 in actuality). They also knew Sirius B was a super dense star rotating on its axis (the force of gravity on Sirius B is apparently 350,000 times greater than Earth's, meaning that on its surface a medium-sized chicken egg would weigh roughly the same as a London double-decker red bus jam-packed with 126 passengers on board). How could the Dogon posses this knowledge displayed in a sand picture hundreds of years before we found out and also without owning telescopes or modern technology?

Critics would argue they must have had people from modern civilizations impart the knowledge with them, or who knows, perhaps those two anthropologists who first made contact in 1931 were desperate for notoriety and just told them contemporary space knowledge. The latter is possible and the former is likely, but doesn't explain how numerous other civilizations and tribes during different time periods describe very similar fish-people from other worlds, one example known to the Babylonians as the Annedoti, meaning repulsive.

The Dogon say there is a third star in the Sirius system, Emma Ya, which has a smaller satellite orbiting around it they call Nyan Tolo, meaning the star of the woman, which two French researchers in 1995 (Daniel Benest and J L Duvet) suggested does exist, but the Hubble Space Telescope has ruled out any bodies larger than a small brown dwarf. If like the moon landings NASA have been lying again and in future years Sirius C's existence is confirmed, it would no doubt settle this perplexing mystery and add great credence to alien encounters.

Life is not only what you make of it but entirely the way you see things, creating your own realities and beliefs based solely on experiences unique to you.

To summarize, seeing life through the microscope to telescope vision of science is like trying to complete a giant crossword given just a few clues. Using every ounce of brainpower has not been nearly enough for the world's greatest minds over many millennia to categorically prove God or Evolution are fact, or that aliens are real for that matter. Perhaps our origin is a question that will end humanity if we could answer it.

Further exploring origin ideas we wonder if there are any overlapping themes to all interpretations and beliefs of life on Earth, like natural common concepts rather than ancestors. One such unifying theory is that of light. Evolution doesn't grow without the sun's rays. God's light is referenced hundreds of times. And witness descriptions of alien and UFO encounters commonly mention super bright lights. Even when people technically die and are brought back to life they talk of bright lights at the end of tunnels. The sun is a gigantic star, central to our solar system, so studying the sun is a good first step to figuring out life on Earth. Ecclesiastes (preacher, 11:7), an Old Testament book of wisdom beautifully says,

"Light is sweet, and it is pleasant for the eyes to see the sun."

Looking at computer simulations of motor proteins makes you feel like a tiny organic machine in the universe constructed like a super complex Lego creation with energy winding into life. And if these double helix biological micro-machine parts landed via asteroids, something still had to make them from somewhere. They are more MECCANO type DNA builds by nature with hinges and some enzymes rotating as fast as 10,000 rpm, rather than random assemblies accidentally clicking cell division into life.

Because we are a mini-universe in ourselves, using your feelings and intuition to ascertain the truth is probably the best measure available. Everyone's energy connects and resonates so perhaps the complex answers to life's greatest metaphysical mysteries have simply been in front of our eyes all along. Believe what your heart tells you because it's only pumping blood around for you. Of all potential explanations, a creator is the clear frontrunner option for the origins of mankind.

THE GOD HYPOTHESIS

Our planet is obviously significantly older than 6,000 years, roughly when Adam was apparently fashioned from dust and Eve was created from one of Adam's ribs, which doesn't sound very scientific even though most strangely, science - previously accused of being the enemy of religion - is now frequently cited as God's work which also helps prove his existence. Scientists estimate the Earth to be about 4.54 billion years old and the Cambrian explosion of animal life appearing in fossils was approximately 541 million years ago.

The Christian Bible (a collection of 66 books between The Hebrew Bible and the New Testament) is a wealth of wisdom full of inspirational stories based on real life events showing you God's light, including supernatural phenomena not everyone agrees with. The part about Noah taking animals two-by-two into his Ark to sustain life during the great flood is captivating and charming, which may have been based upon three hypothetical flood scenarios known as the Black Sea deluge.

Jesus Christ is the star of the Bible and everything he said was great, inspirational and correct. He hit all the relevant psychological and philosophical nails available, right on the head. After a few thousand years we still desperately need his oracular words to guide us or we'll fall because few people have the balls to find their soul on their own without a prophet holding their hand.

God is making a big comeback because the science world is showing it's truly corrupt colours.

So why do people believe in God or gods? When we're born we are totally reliant on our parents and this feeling never goes away in adulthood. Our genetic make-up is programmed to worship a pyramid hierarchy. It's in our genes to look up to people and keep looking up until we see no faults in the one at the top. God and heaven were once imagined to be in the sky above the clouds or beyond the firmament, but now we know through science that He and heaven aren't residing there as previously believed. Because of our Christmas tree type social hierarchy and persistent desire for parental care and advice, we constantly look for and appoint leaders, then elevate their status to help us feel protected. And when those leaders fail, people fantasize about better ones, creating idyllic alternatives who possess supreme powers to remove their real life corrupt leaders causing them misery and suffering. We could call this survival instinct and imprinting anomaly the Superman Syndrome.

It's a fact that humans are delusion dreamers. We need to always feel like someone is fighting our corner, like a knight in shining armour, a mentor guiding you through tough times, or some people even believe guardian angels have their back. We're designed to look for psychological help almost as much as looking for food. Comic book characters are hugely popular because people like to imagine the baddies being crushed by greater powers than we possess. By a strange coincidence, the bad guys are often ugly and the goodies are frequently attractive so we can fantasize more about our favourite saviour superheroes. God could be viewed as the greatest comic book character the world has ever seen.

You have more power to change the world than you think.

Most humans love to respect higher ups, the establishment, the elite, the cream of society and lots of people have always been totally obsessed with celebrity role models, giving them godlike status. Sheeple and groupies will do anything to be like or sleep with their idols just because they're fucking famous. It's embarrassingly pathetic how far humans go to find, project and revere a god on earth. Stone statues and oil portraits are another form of pseudo-parental idolisation. We call priests Father and title others Sir, Dame, Lord, champion, ruler, chief, etc, in a persistent scouting out for new parental figures to admire and protect us. We all want a powerful mummy or daddy.

It's not a bizarre coincidence Father Christmas is named Father and looks like God either because God is viewed by many atheists as the adult version of Santa Claus. Santa gives children the promise of joy and adults lie to make that happen for the good of the children. God is the ultimate parent and leader substitute. His teachings are amazing, perfect, uncannily everything you ever wanted in a supreme, omnipresent being. Humans are so self-obsessed, if they were to imagine an omnipotent, all-powerful deity it would definitely be created in the image of Man. Perhaps God didn't make himself look like us for our benefit, rather humans imagined him that way because that's what we'd most like to see. As the French Enlightenment philosopher and poet Voltaire wrote,

"If God did not exist, it would be necessary to invent him."

To most people, believing in God is a necessary survival mechanism and uniting community force. The fact we need fatherly direction from above doesn't mean God or gods are real though. Maybe God is a practical way to create hope where none exists; a human manifestation of our deepest dreams and desires; not only a figment of our furtive imaginations but a longing to receive more love. The psychological fact remains that humans like to feel protected and literally can't stand thinking they are alone in the universe. Without God you are left with just yourself and that's not enough for most people. We need divine leadership, not loneliness and if that means lying to ourselves then so be it.

The idea of not being able to fathom the complexities of human origins is an unacceptable hole in knowledge. We constantly attribute meaning where there is none because we won't accept the idea our existence is meaningless and life is all for nothing. Life is life, it just happens. You have kids or you don't and you die. We're so afraid of death and nothingness that humans create a whole fiction around afterlife. Gravestones of our loved ones help us grieve but the deceased person most likely couldn't give a fuck because they're dead. Our mortality scares most people shitless. A great many religious flocks despise the idea there may be nothing after death because it's not a nice imagining. It's okay for there to be nothing though. It will help you live your life better knowing it's a one-time ride. You don't have to fear dying. You're not that important. Regardless, these unripe thoughts deny the life-long calling millions of people feel towards a divine creator which could simply be because there is one.

It's a tad awkward saying you've spoken to God without sounding an incy-wincy bit mad.

When faced with a daily barrage of evil policies and Draconian measures, a belief in God is the last bastion of hope for many; a promise and great way to rally support to defeat the forces of evil working away in the background like leeches and parasites draining your power. However, atheists conclude this doesn't make it true though and for all the good that personal religious belief does, they think believing in something we can't incontrovertibly prove exists is the precise reason we keep getting fooled by evil intentions. It's fine if you want to believe in something incorporeal or invisible because it makes you feel better and gives your life meaning, but don't complain about other people who do exactly the same when it doesn't suit your narrative, like Covidians who believe the covid pandemic is real, despite all scientific and logical evidence saying otherwise, because their fear can't face the depopulation agenda truth, just like some religious people can't face their universal insignificance and possible lack of heavenly protection. As the polemicist Voltaire wrote,

"The true triumph of reason is that it enables us to get along with those who do not possess it."

Humanity won't move forward onto the next level of consciousness as long as we keep believing in anything that makes us feel psychologically comfortable whether it's real or not. God could just be wishful thinking. And why is God not a woman, some misandrist feminists may ask. Perhaps because wealthy men controlled society and subjugated women in Jesus' time, the cabal decided to make their instrument for oppression and knowledge hoarding in the likeness of a man to maintain the status quo. Let's further enter the mind and thoughts of atheists for balance and fairness because if you don't walk in another person's shoes you won't know how well your shoes fit.

Science is based on trial and error using instruments, method and logic, whereas religion is primarily based on emotions, the soul and ancient text. Humans mainly react to their emotions, therefore science is given very little respect or acknowledgement in comparison, explaining why the cult of covid sheep ignore scientific facts in favour of fear. We are simply led by our emotions - mainly fear and love, and they're indefinable. Logic rarely overrides our feelings and fears. Even if you really try, you can't shake off the feeling that God exists either because repeating cultural concepts ingrained in society never go away, because of the superman syndrome, or perhaps because He or a divine being does exist. And just the same as how people blatantly lie to defend the covid myth, for thousands of years people created superstitions to defend the unproven God theory. We all understand the reasons why, but on a logical, material level we appreciate it seems bizarre to some people believing in something that may not exist. But that's humans for you, they'll fight wars over nothing, murder people defending the invisible and scream out in jubilant crowds watching less fortunate starving people hang for petty crimes.

As tyranny creeps closer day by day, putting your money on God in Pascal's Wager is looking increasingly like a sensible option.

To the logical mind there is plenty of doubt of God's existence, so perhaps the correct assumption is that He does not until more is known. Surely it's rational to sit on the agnostic's fence and let your thoughts waver like a hung jury if you can't prove to the opposition you are right. Or perhaps you're done with diplomacy because life's too short to go around in circles. Let's remind ourselves, the most brilliant hoaxes, cons, psyops and delusions are based on 100% lies because no-one can ever find evidence to disprove their narrative, so everything imaginable could be used to reinforce the deception.

Sometimes the one true God works in so many mysterious ways it's almost like he doesn't exist and when people ask for his help he never comes so they have to pretend anything slightly beneficial that happens was a clear sign from God instead of just something good happening or a friend helping out because they saw them struggling. Once you have a mystifying, ambiguous entity, it's easy to attribute anything and everything to its existence. The non-existent Covid-19 disease has every illness under the sun flying its banner. The more unknown and invisible, the greater its power to deceive people desperate for hope and to end cruel government restrictions.

Asking anyone to prove beyond questionable doubt the Invisible Man, Covid-19, aliens and planet Nibiru exists is an impossible task, therefore we could easily conclude they are all mere theories, not facts. If a person can't provide any concrete or creditable evidence from any angle that they are right, then it seems hypocritical telling someone they are wrong simply based on firm hunches, strong personal feelings or even voices inside your head. The onus for any theorist is to prove their belief, not to tell people they don't understand, otherwise they'd be no rhyme nor reason to anything.

Why does the God concept get a freer pass than other origin of Man beliefs which are often disrespectfully scrutinized and derided, dare we offend religion. Millions of religious people believe that different faiths are wrong because they're not the same as theirs, which is wrong in itself and not true. It's fallacious reasoning and special pleading when everything but your belief needs a cause to exist. It's also incorrect and insulting suggesting an atheist has no soul otherwise they would worship God. Perhaps because an atheist has a soul they don't need to invent a deity to worship and god-fearing people are trying to compensate for what they lack inside? Either argument could have merit.

We sadly often witness a real intellectual, arrogant paradox and egotism in some people saying they *know* God exists but can't provide a shred of scientific, empirical or testable evidence. We all have our theories, proving them is the big problem. A Bible-basher accusing an atheist of spiritual autism, hatred and brain deficiency is not the kindness and love Jesus promotes. And how can anyone hate what they don't believe exists?

Two can play the patronising game. Saying God exists because your soul connects with him, or that God *is* your soul, is no more compelling evidence than someone else saying their path to enlightenment revealed to them a much deeper spiritual level than praying to God offers. Religion fills a loneliness void but if you were enlightened you'd never feel lonely and perhaps if you had a true belief in yourself as a force for good and capable of being a leader, you wouldn't need faith in anyone or anything but yourself.

Suggesting atheists who walk the wide path need to be weeded out is no less offensive than the atheist insisting religious belief is a type of delusional mental illness. God loves a trier, not an arsehole. Surely any faith which discourages you questioning things is more of a dictatorial cult. God could be an elaborate representation of the feeling of hope and peace of mind which has be hijacked by satanists to control the masses for thousands of years. Many atheists feel we should just accept that God – in the intellectually tangible, accessible form humans have created – is unlikely to be real, so it's best to take the great lessons from the Bible and stick to them religiously. The Bible is certainly the greatest self-help book ever.

God beliefs come in many forms from lots of different and deeply interesting philosophical directions, so to merely claim

He or divine creators do not exist from a scientific or material perspective is limiting and may lead us away from the truth. Billions of religious people simply can't be wrong can they? Most people still wrongly believe we went to the moon; that governments are working for our best interests; that your vote counts; that fact checkers are not full of shit government shills; that Muslims believe they get rewarded for hurting disbelievers; that Osama Bin Laden was responsible for 9/11; that the media is impartial; that asymptomatic Covid-19 happens; that Western governments are benevolent; that Oswald killed Kennedy; that Hitler and Marilyn Monroe committed suicide; and that an iceberg sunk the Titanic. But most of these common, dim-witted conclusions are caused by a simple, lazy lack of basic research and reading, curiosity and thought. The idea of God is ancient, eternal and passes through the smallest atoms in the universe into a celestial dimension of its own. You can't fairly dismiss what you don't feel inside. The rhythm of the universe is within us all.

The Top 5 complaints made by atheists about God and religion are:

1. Why would a loving, all-powerful God allow millions of people to die in wars, die of illness before their time, or starve to death, be enslaved, etc, without divine intervention? Surely this makes God cruel to let many innocent children suffer and die in pain. Why be born with original sin? Does not God provide an excuse for demented maniacs and psychopaths to torture people? In the name of their snake god, Kukulan, the Ancient Mayans (starting from at least

the Classic period around 250 AD) used a wide variety of horrific sacrificial methods; such as cutting the still-beating heart from their victims, straightforward decapitation, a ritual of shooting arrows at their heart and chucking sacrifices into a deep sinkhole. These power-crazed nutcases even danced on the meat suits of skinned victims and also ate their organs. Way back then and nowadays, at grassroots level where God is really needed, it's hard to tell if he makes any impact at all apart from raising people's spirits and finding solace with fellow believers. The masses could *really* use a divine creator stepping in to help out in desperate times, like a parent stopping their children fighting. These are valid points, but easily countered by reminding ourselves we have a free will and choice to stop the globalist devils before they destroy society as we know it. We could argue that God made us too sheep-like to fight back against the forces of evil, but that's what righteousness and courage is about.

2. Is God not just a convenient, made-made concept to allow sinners to be forgiven? The saying, *if you can't do the time, don't do the crime,* is more like what God is offering with sufferance, purgatory and redemption, not total forgiveness into the kingdom of heaven just by saying sorry about that. One could go as far to suggest that if you have never done a person wrong, don't lack spiritual awareness and have faith in yourself, you would not remotely need God, but no-one is flawless or develops supreme confidence from nowhere without failure and experience. Religion gives millions of people the spirit and self-belief to fight evil which can't be a bad thing in my book and this is my book. Christianity is the perfect antidote to, escape hatch from and way to unmask evil.

3. God and religion seem to be all about controlling people which is the antithesis of the spiritual freedom it preaches. The amount of pain and suffering committed in the name of God over the centuries is unforgivable. If you were to create the perfect fear-mongering, emotional blackmail scheme to keep people in check and do as they are told, then the idea that good people will experience peace and love in heaven, and bad people will suffer pain and torture for eternity in hell is the pinnacle of psychological manipulation. After all, Heaven and Hell have never been located on the map, but if you do wonder what hell is like go to McDonalds.

Is God worship not just another mind controlling cult? In very religious countries like Italy, America and India, religious skeptics could find themselves unpopular and ostracised. Religious cynics and other minority tribes can be treated with disrespect and distain in many countries for no fair reason just because they didn't join a popular club. God will strike you down if you don't follow his rulebook. Very few people can resist peer pressure, especially when you may lose job opportunities. You can receive jail for blasphemy or even the death penalty in over a dozen Muslim countries just for being an infidel or *kafir*. Criticise Darwinism or alien theories and you gain applause. Criticise

God and you receive insults and digs, or it falls on deaf ears because you're criticizing a coordinated belief system which could be the only saviour and salvation of all time. People find it hard to separate reality from hope and often confuse hope with intuition. Lots of atheists are done with delusional people projecting their fears onto others because of their apparent ignorance. Also, the very people who should be promoting altruism and respect can rapidly turn into a shouting mob defending their cast-iron beliefs. Haven't we heard that before from the cult of covid who are like putty in the devil's hands. Blind faith is fanatical thinking which is close-minded and dangerous. The god-squad can get really nasty, sly and backstabbing under the delusional belief they are superior. Surely superior people don't need a philosophical leader. Many hearts confirm that God exists, but many brains conclude he doesn't.

In addition, why are so many religious people so reluctant to discuss their faith or hear about other people's beliefs and opinions? The lack of tolerance for other beliefs is concerning. Religion herds people into cages while simultaneously saying it's releasing your soul like a captive bird into the wild. Questioning the Bible narrative is deemed heresy. The whole idea of God is you never question his existence or teachings and in return he offers you spiritual eternity which does seem a bit culty. Submit to the will of God otherwise you won't be rewarded sounds a lot like a threat, not a welcoming invitation. And what God are we talking about anyway. Hinduism scriptures claim there are 33 *Koti* (core) gods (there's that number again). The truth is usually little bits of everything that shines to create a sun.

4. Why are all the famous, high-up preachers, bishops, clergy, ministers, etc, who spread the word of Jesus Christ around the world, dripping with obscene amounts of gold? Jesus made it very clear owning excessive personal wealth while others suffer poverty and starvation was morally indefensible. If you're a materialist you're not a follower of Jesus. Usury was once a crime but now the central banking system holds whole countries to ransom. With nearly two and half billion worldwide followers, the Christian Church is obviously one of the biggest money earners around. It's *very* big business. The Vatican representing the Catholic Church owns countless billions in money, gold, art and property, yet around 10,000 children die every day from undernutrition. Nothing can defend this immoral division of wealth and the actions of corrupt people who hijack a good cause. There's also theodicy. Think of all the well-known charitable organisations who have been exposed many times for clearing out the coffers by paying exorbitant CEO and management wages before a small fraction of the money kindly donated goes to the needy at the end of the chain of charity theft. However, you can rightly blame church organisations and crooked individuals for avarice and fraud, but not the word of God which means well.

5. Why does the church have a long history of paedophiliac priests and does a lot to sweep these sick crimes under the carpet but takes very little action to punish the perpetrators? Priests are often strange people in between bouts of paedophilia. Rather than being yet another one of many large cult organisations knee-deep in paedophilia, the church has frequently been accused of being the epicentre of child abuse, paedophile rings and even child trafficking, therefore that's another reason the atheist wants nothing to do with God. Beware, when you pay money into a belief system to help spread the word of your God, you may also be unknowingly entering into an organisation run by gold and silver obsessed maniacs who fuck and sell kids for sport. Again, we must point the finger at the sickos not the saviours. Money corrupts people and people invented money. As the Epistle to the Ephesians 6:12 from the King James Version says,

"For we wrestle not against flesh and blood, but against principalities, against powers, against the rulers of the darkness of this world, against spiritual wickedness in high places."

Intelligent design, the Fibonacci sequence and DNA are buzz-phrases being thrown around with zealous enthusiasm. However, the idea that the golden ratio and genetics count as undeniable evidence of intelligent design made by a divine creator is nothing short of a mad leap of faith, even though it could be true. Every living organism has to be made of something and have a structure of some kind. Naturally the most successful designs become the most popular until unifying themes run throughout all living things as says the theory of evolution before religion kidnapped that fundamental idea of how life grows. Obviously, of all the successful functioning proteins created, the least efficient ones die out first. On the one hand many religious people insist science is rubbish because it doesn't take into account the unknown spirit world, the soul or God, and on the other hand they say science helps prove there is a God. It's a hell of a jump to scientifically or religiously conclude that just because everything has a building block, a code or strain of sorts, therefore a God put all the pieces together. That's like seeing a childlike painting and assuming a child painted it.

Some religious people have a tendency to attribute anything and everything to God without logic or reason, willed on by their admirable devotion. As more and more evidence contradicting the Bible is recognised, religious organisations have cleverly mixed up their origin story with science and even with evolution as well to keep an ancient philosophy alive. Science is trail and error and doesn't claim to being anything but that, whereas religion frequently alludes to a final, uncorrupted, unquestionable conclusion. One is flexible, the latter is set in stone and as time moves on we see the description and interpretations of God altering to suit new discoveries and popular narratives. Nevertheless, why should we trust science when nearly every time you thoroughly look into their claims it's all lies to get grant money.

Regardless, when looking over the human condition and our ability to harmonize with nature we fail to see how humans have appointed themselves the definition of intelligent.

Sacrificing and exploiting people into a slave based system is not intelligent design in action. What we mean is people are slightly more intelligent and sophisticated than dogs who lick their balls and arseholes all day long. We start wars, destroy civilisations, slaughter most animals and repeat this madness over thousands of years, ritualistically playing out the same disappointing and cruel stories in a continuous trap of our own making with little promise of breaking the chain of greed. That's not intelligence. Intelligent design is harmonious.

If people didn't listen to their government or television we wouldn't be in this mess.

The universe is a never-ending loop of molecules inside molecules working on repetition and replication. The brain is a universe in itself. We are all biological machines made from miniscule organic mechanisms you can't see with the naked eye. Much of life is a chain reaction from multiple states to solids. When something dies, new life takes its place. Sperm finds the ovum and grows, and pollen fertilizes a compatible pistil. Masculine and feminine, yin and yang, positive and negative ions. Maybe planet Earth is a seed and we - the animals and plants - are its nutrients. Could Adam and Eve represent the yin and yang, and the seeds for all life come from the Garden of Eden.

Because we can obviously only think like humans, it's logical for us to conclude the world is a flat zoo for a higher being to nurture animals and us in the perfect habitat and incubator for humanity to grow and thrive. Looking at empirical evidence we see how easy it is for governments to program nearly everyone's minds. In fact, it's so easily done we have to entertain the idea people are a composite of little biological machines linked together, perhaps not evolved, rather produced somehow by a divine creator to balance out the planet's energy or animal kingdom. Our brains are hardwired to react the same to everything. Maybe our genetic structure itself is the matrix.

How comes this relatively small planet in a corner of a universe is teeming with life, so perfectly positioned to the life giving sun and with the right conditions for growth, it's almost like we humans have been handed the house keys to do as we please. Surely there are other similar planets and life forms out there, and if so have the creatures visited us without us knowing and how were they created too. It's highly likely huge chucks and wide expanses of knowledge about humanity are completely skew-whiff or just plain wrong. Many advanced civilizations had almost certainly existed before ours, yet were destroyed by nature, asteroids or themselves and buried under millions of years of planetary changes.

In our desperation to answer the unknown we imagine humans must have landed here from somewhere else, or there's an overwhelming feeling we were just plonked on this planet by forces beyond our comprehension which could be because it's the truth in both cases. The universe might be nothing like what we picture from the pictures we've been shown since childhood, or from our own eyes and mathematical and physics calculations. It's a possibility the universe is not expanding, being a sum of all its parts instead and we are looping round inside a huge dome or sphere. The only real science and astronomy we have is from some ancient and modern parts of history and amateur enthusiasts telling the truth because you can be damn sure the authorities aren't telling the truth about space.

It makes logical sense that life on Earth came from the earth but the fact we haven't even got close to proving our origin shows logic to be very limited when dealing with spiritual matters. Humans suffer great mental conflict if decisions aren't made, if questions remain unanswered, if conclusions aren't drawn, be they true or convenient balderdash. The least knowledge we have, the more need to lie to ourselves. We prefer a neatly wrapped-up lie over a scattered conjectures littering our minds. God is what most people want to hear. Evolution is a tidy idea too, even exquisite one could argue but likely wrong. And science is as limited as blind faith.

Perhaps the enlightened agnostic mind feels no pressure or requirement to follow a faith system because they truly believe in themselves and the power of nature. Nature is real, forgiving, tangible and healing. Many nonbelievers and faithless find their way to higher spiritual and metaphysical dimensions, even parallel universes, without the aid of scripture, choosing meditation over prayer. Whatever gets you there dude. Some lucky people are just born godly and don't need to find anything to enhance their spiritual development as divine conduits of universal truth.

Blind faith doesn't lead to a higher spiritual connection with almighty powers. Instead, unquestioning faith limits your mental outlook and corners you into defending some indefensible positions which is the birth of delusion, stopping you from seeing the bigger picture and accessing the most profound of truthful insights. Covidians and similar quasi-religious cults also don't like to be questioned because they've been led astray and don't have the right answers. Truth always answers every question or accusation without breaking a sweat or feeling threatened. If you switch off from hearing alternative views you're not open-minded and miss opportunities for wisdom. Be as open as the air which travels the world.

Religious people are frequently referred to as sheep, not in a godly way but derogatorily. Some atheists believe religious flocks huddle together because they're weak and brainwashed by corrupt religious organisations. Yes, lots of lost and mentally ill people turn to God in desperation - falling prey to religious scams - but in reverse many people suffering from mental disturbance lose their faith too and are exploited. Plus it's natural to try to stabilise a chaotic life.

One underrated and significant point the covid plandemic shows is that far from being sheeple, many of the people who saw straight through the covid lie were religious which surprised atheists and didn't fit their narrative that religion can put a spell on you, so you can't see beyond the concept of God and when people feel powerless they imagine power. Many Christian's straightforward ability to spot cunning covid propaganda for what it is and look at unspoilt science data objectively, clearly showed that religious belief does not veil or obscure your mind from the pattern of truth, far from it - enhancing reality and helping believers identify sources of evil. This religious grip on reality, being one step ahead of the pack, gives credence to God's existence. As Matthew 10:16 says,

"I am sending you out like sheep among wolves. Therefore be as shrewd as snakes and as innocent as doves."

You can't possibly understand the darkest depths of madness by reading a self-help book, passing a psychology degree or listening to a victim of insanity. Only personal experience can give you the answers you seek. The same goes for you finding God. Surrendering to a God isn't a defeat, you're just saving yourself time. The God hypothesis is a survival mechanism buried deep inside our soul and linked to our genetic predispositions. It's against human nature to reject what you really need. God exists as a living embodiment in every person full of goodwill for their fellow man.

We are currently facing the forces of evil and darkness on an unprecedented scale - way more monstrous than even World War II - where the same cult who heavily profited from that war are making another attempt at world domination. People are losing their sense of reason and ability to debate without insults and hatred because they feel threatened by a society which has stabbed them in the back. Therefore right now, the world needs devout Christians who genuinely follow the word of Jesus Christ as much as we need oxygen and all other religions too opposing the inevitable, ominous darkness coming that *we can* defeat if we all stick together, defend the truth and be courageous. There comes a point where you have to stop caring about the outcome and do what you can to stand against tyranny.

We're heading for bad times but this certainly doesn't mean we have to stop living or having fun among ourselves.

Regarding God, Evolution and aliens, I conclude that your private beliefs are your business and no-one else's because how can anybody describe your life experiences and feelings better than you. As a strong believer in using one's intuition to connect with reality to find the ultimate truth behind everything, I cannot ignore this innate, primordial feeling of a guiding spirit beyond one's consciousness telling you you're going to be okay – also telling you there is a divine creator. Millions of people swear if you open your emotions up you'll find a calling to God that doesn't leave no matter what you believe: they simply *know* in their hearts without need for articulation and who is anyone to question the love someone feels for anyone or anything.

Are not most enlightened people held back describing their profound experiences and wisdom by the limitations of language and semantics, as the sound and rhythm of the universe, and the light of emotional knowledge are omnipresent truths – more beautiful tones than flowery words. All enlightened souls have a powerful, ever-present calling to the same universal beacon of hope, resonating selfless, eternal beliefs beyond our cognition and corporeal attachment. The soul's energy is you, which no doubt grows through other forms after your physical passing. As the Serbian-American inventor, engineer and futurist Nikola Tesla wrote,

"The Buddhist expresses it in one way, the Christian in another, but both say the same: We are all one."

Believing in God is an important psychological process and holy stepping stone towards gaining the enlightenment of undiluted truth and learning how to root out evil from its multifarious disguises. Other people have a deep spiritual connection with nature only, where every fibre of their being resonates over hills and far beyond. They feel the heartbeat of the universe inside the most private corridors and profound experiences in their psyche and bones.

A spiritual presence echoes centuries of ancient pilgrimage footsteps and the palimpsest of cultured wisdom which seeks peace, love and truth and stands against bullying, narcissism and falsehood. Examining the heartwood of enlightenment we see an uncomplicated dimension with no fixed abode, freely travelling through space. Many good and bad overlapping and separate layers of consciousness are magnetised towards the enlightened mind, all looking for self-improvement in one way or another.

Most people get stuck at level one selfishness and materialism, and struggle to find any significant, eternal meaning to life and therefore remain slightly dissatisfied and unhappy their whole lives - often due to being mentally bone idle. Cognitive laziness, apathy and putting your head in the sand through fear are some of the biggest modern day sins. For the rest of us who can be bothered to question rules and regulations, and who want to return to natural reality, the classic steps taken towards enlightenment are thus:

1. Step one is mental suffering: surfeiting; social anxiety; your subconscious battling brainwashed thoughts; hurt with relationship greed by going out of your league; egotism (not to be confused with high confidence); wracked with jealousy; overthinking; overeating; whatever your vice or main weakness which brings you crashing down to earth.

2. Step two is managing and conquering some personal problems and weaknesses with determination and fortitude.

3. Step three is wanting to break free from the matrix and needing a higher purpose. Deprogramming your mind from propaganda filth and lies, and seeing the sheep for the obsequious cretins they really are.

4. Opening your mind to religious and/or spiritual beliefs to develop your emotional intelligence if you haven't already done so. Bonding with nature is an important part of this step.

5. Thinking about the universe, turning everything on its head and going down all rabbit holes that come your way. A search for truth and acceptance of the social fakery we live in.

6. Successfully rejecting and detaching your mind from human systems and problems with a positive outlook on your destiny, adopting a productive focus, passion and direction in life regardless of obstacles. This will certainly mean not having many friends and experiencing months of solitude as you convert from a product of society to a free thinking organism in nature.

7. Battling the forces of evil. Confronting evil people - hopefully one at a time - and winning out.

8. To not keep fluctuating or backtracking through some or all of the previous steps, achieving a timeless calm.

If it's in your heart then it's true.

However we arrived on planet Earth and whatever our collective purpose, it's of lesser importance than learning how best to survive. Anyone with a moderately functioning brain realizes that contemporary society is an illusion and virtually everything we're officially told is a blatant lie to disguise corporate crimes and deep state financial and sexual deviancies. Billions of sheep still don't get the basic idea we live in a global economy with a worldwide political agenda and your country's flag means absolutely nothing to the New World Order whose global companies and banks have silently declared war on billions of innocent folk without most people even knowing what's going on. It's not a case of they're taking over because they've already taken over after placing thousands of cult members in prominent positions of power in a calculated and nefarious attack on our previously, relatively free way of living where for once many of the people owned their own homes and made free choices.

Speedily done behind the red curtain of spurious emergencies, these locust type billionaires are buying up millions of acres of farmland and as many buildings as possible across the world with the intention of crashing the economy, then reviving it once they own everything and have full control over your life. You won't be able to breathe without first having your mouth QR code scanned if people don't rise up in defence of basic human rights and natural law. This is no longer just a global economic dictatorship, but an attempt to take slices out of our souls, piece by piece until all we have left is obedience. Keep strong and united against tyranny and we will successfully resist these evil monsters together. Evil billionaires are just people. If they feel the power of the mob they will run like every other one of us. If the people don't take drastic action against tyranny in the next decade we'll eventually be no better off than Roman slaves. As William Wallace (1270-1305 AD) the famous Scottish military leader said,

"Deep in the human heart
The fire of justice burns;
A vision of a world renewed
Through radical concern."

A big part of the NWO agenda is to destroy Christianity because that's the true foundation of decency and happiness. There is no quality of life if you live in servitude. You either follow the crowd or obey your conscience. Your unelected leaders put a cage around you for a fictitious emergency, then unlock the door at random times and we're somehow supposed to be grateful. Don't play their gaslighting game.

Ignore all nonsensical and cruel rules that stop you being free. Dictators drill holes in your lifeboat then sell you corks to keep afloat for a while and then expect you to say thanks.

See society as the superficial con it is and you'll stop being afraid of its ability to harm you.

Tyranny always starts with the tyrant pretending to look out for your safety while his army digs graves for dissenting freedom fighters at nighttime to the shriek of a raven's prophecy. Every government lie you believe takes you one step closer to digging your own grave. When you lose hope the enemy gains power. Fear will always be the greatest weapon the enemies of freedom have if you give it to them. Evil people thrive on your fear and die with your bravery. Let no man dictate how you choose to live your life. This is the time, before it's too late for everyone with different beliefs and ideas on life to unite in one common goal to stop what are becoming The Fourth Reich from going full Nazi on us. The only human rights you have is what you're prepared to fight for. You can live in mortal fear about things that don't exist or see your life as an incredible journey through the universe. And your number one responsibility is to protect children by building them a future worth having.

In the early hours of the morning when all is quiet, you can hear the clock and your mind ticking, and sense in the silence, courage in your beating heart.

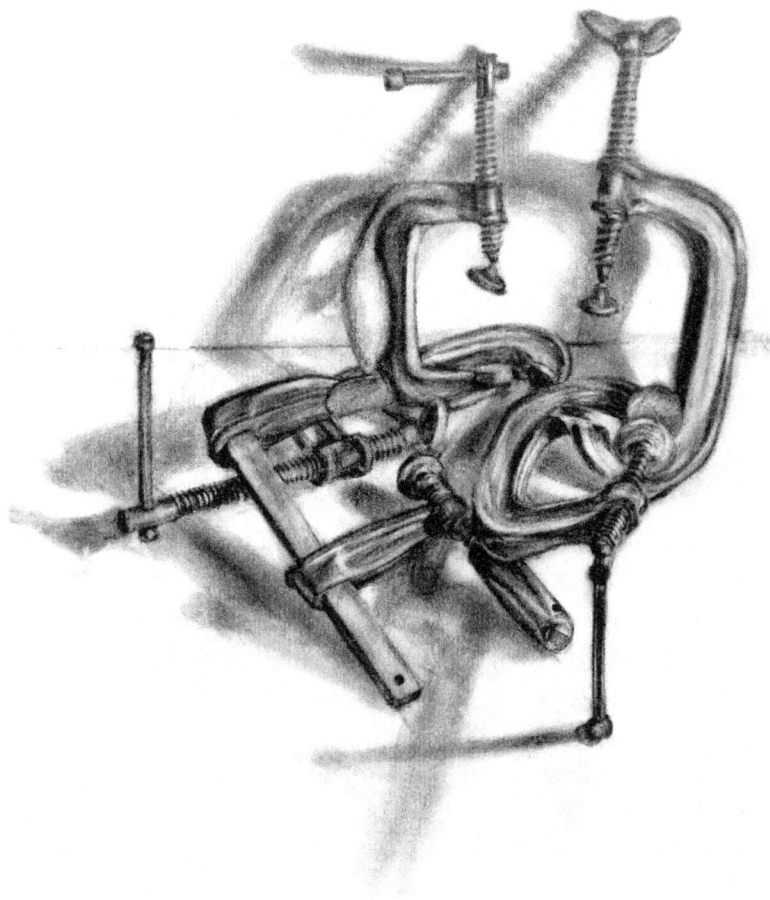

Turning the screw.

A virtual world

A virtual world is not a world worth having. At some point in life the majority of humans get greedy and/or try to elevate themselves above their upbringing and background. And about one third of people become embarrassed or even ashamed of their own commoner parents, or ditch their school friends who haven't done so well, or distance themselves from their family in order to find suitable peers to create a new, higher class narrative for themselves – more money being the main motivation.

Nice can become nasty oh so easily if greed is injected into an ambitious psyche, like gangrene spreading foul pestilence. Most people have a perpetual desire to be excessively admired and loved or revered – even if they don't know or admit it. Or perhaps you just want to look cool to fit in through fear of isolation. It's natural to want to improve yourself, yet it's a slippery path believing you are better than anyone else. You certainly won't find character in clothes or cars.

Few people can transcend all the weaknesses they inherit. Winners often learn how to thrive within their limitations. Winning is keeping as much life alive as possible. As long as money rules in most people's minds we'll remain trapped in a money pit mentality. Finding a non-materialistic free thinker nowadays is the perfect definition of a needle in a haystack. Robots will make people obsolete. Technology helps us at first then replaces you. Artificial intelligence is just another way to depopulate and enslave.

The idea there are too many people in the world to be sustainable is one of the biggest myths around. Too many rich assholes, yes, but not people.

Apart from fear which is a reaction, throughout most of history our top societal nemeses have been a lust for money and seeking social status; two intermeshed and confused weaknesses in a chicken and egg scenario which shape the social matrix we operate in. By *status* we don't mean the vehicles for differentiation like fashion and bling. I am talking about our desperate innate need to shuffle up and down the pecking order until everybody else has put you in your place. Status seeking has become a common obsession because when governments narrow people's options and wages, people feel more trapped, so try harder to be free by stretching reality, usually maxing-out their credit cards and pawning goods. With less cash to splash, people use deception to convince others they are social climbers rather than look uncool by sensibly living within one's means. Another common status seeking tactic is marrying and divorcing a number of times for financial gain; seeing a relationship more as an asset stripping opportunity to travel lots and buy nice things, rather than a profound loving experience. Children and society are commonly the casualties of gold-digging vacuousness.

The desire to mate is incredibly strong, yet the urge to display and impress just comes in second place after greed rears its ugly head over the winning line because food is more desired than sex. To begin, we have an individual impulse and then everyone else lets us know if that is within their rules. From time immemorial the person who can bring home the most bacon is admired the most. The meat in ancient time or money now is the greed impulse, shortly followed by a desire for repeat abundance which develops the status. What drives us is what comes first and we seek status via humans' Achilles heel, greed.

Before a toddler has to face social rules, they are usually given much leeway to make mistakes. With ample freedom the child will always try to get the maximum outcome in their favour (more milk, attention, toys, etc). They take gifts of love and food for granted. As they grow, society begins to impose more and more constraints most unfairly. Greed says 'go' and society says 'no' until the young adult is finally whipped into shape and learns to search for 'yes' responses and permissions.

Most people haven't got the confidence to be themselves, so they seek daily affirmations from the herd and can't wait to show off what hot shit they pretend to be or pay the penalty of being shunned. Characterful individuals are frequently swamped out by the bird in the hand brigade. Status is mostly achieved if the sheep majority want to be like you, confirming what they want to hear. Also, because sheeple are fickle and cowardly, sometimes they'll support a renegade freedom fighter to do the dirty work and thinking for them if a government starves everyone into submission.

The very same type of stubborn anarchists the sheep choose to ostracise on a daily basis are those they secretly admire - like having a back-up sexual partner just in case. There are 3 main currencies for people: inheritance, beauty and willpower. Those factors shall dictate your standing inside the matrix. Interestingly, the origin of the word matrix from Old French *matrice* means womb, uterus, and from Latin mātrix meaning pregnant animal, and in Late Latin māter means mother.

It's like The Truman Show but in reverse and you're just one thinking person watching all the clueless people around you who don't realise they're being played like puppets.

So what is the matrix, the frequently used phrase describing the inner workings of society, made mega-popular by the 1999 film The Matrix. Surely society can't actually be like that entertaining and thought provoking teenager's sci-fi action movie where Keanu Reaves' computer hacker character Neo embarks on a journey of truth, discovering the whole of society is a lie because people live in a computer simulation while their energy is being harvested. The more you understand society, the less that movie premise seems far-fetched, especially as we enter a dystopian digital age where the human body is going to be injected, infiltrated and installed with numerous electronic devices and nanotechnology, having mortifying consequences for a slave society that may not be able to fight back like they used to.

Being capable of turning people off with the press of a button can't be a good thing.

In fact, it's frightening how many apocalyptic and dystopian novels and movies are coming to life nowadays: George Orwell's 1984 being the winner because he was a benign cult member and knew exactly what was going to happen as was Aldous Huxley and his spin on build back better in 1932 with Brave New World, possibly not quoted from Miranda in The Tempest but instead a nod to the New World Order beginning a new war on the world, previously using Hitler as a their pawn who turned against and outsmarted them, most likely escaping, not committing suicide.

To annul the fear by familiarising the plebs with the horrors that the NWO psychos most graciously have in store for us, the powers that be even commission books, TV series and movies to live out their dystopian fantasies so the people slowly get used to their evil plans and systems coming true. TV and movie scripts condition weak minds into subconscious compliance. Notable strangely prophetic films and books include We by Yevgeny Zamyatin, Demolition Man, The Omega Man, The Handmaid's Tale, Children of Men by P. D. James, V for Vendetta, Fahrenheit 451, Logan's Run, Soylent Green, Gattaca, Lord of the Flies, A Clockwork Orange, Dead Plague, Contagion, The Marburg Virus and Life Without Birth by Stanley Johnson, Atlas Shrugged by Ayn Rand, The Hunger Games, Animal Farm, The Island, Equilibrium, Total Recall, They Live, 12 Monkeys, I Am Legend and oddly some The Simpsons episodes too. And possibly even The Terminator which reveals the NWO obsession with robotic control of mankind, known for slipping subliminal messages into television programmes and adverts for all kinds of nasty reasons beyond just selling a product to brainwash tired people. Everything the happens in the matrix is pre-planned. You have as much free speech as you like until thousands of people start listening. Society has become so weird it wouldn't be a surprise to find out we're extras in an antiutopian movie for popcorn eating alien's entertainment.

The entire world of smart thinkers are still stunned by how sheep-like most people are being, it's like they're a different species.

CITADEL OF ANTS

To ascertain the true depth, brainwashing and coercion the system has already exercised over virtually everyone's bar-coded lives, we first need to separate the natural hierarchical process of successful creatures from technology and warlike psychology because super societies create their own problematic matrix. Cities are huge lumps of clay and concrete dividing pockets of people, and learning about ant behaviour oddly gives us a great insight into how mega-groups, metropolises and city mentalities are formed. As we see from ants, gigantic groups uncomfortably speed up the pace of life to a frenzied state until the workload exceeds average physical capabilities creating new diseases and problems unique to mega-cities. Some large ant colonies have major problems identifying their residents' authenticity as well.

Ants are funny little creatures, surprisingly like humans. Look into the tiny world of ants and we see disturbing social resemblances to our own species. Perhaps humans are not the great thinkers and creators we believe. Is the definition of a great species one that can physically defeat more creatures than any other, or support more life? Ants seem to overtake and pillage areas they occupy like we do, so it's lucky they're so small because pound for pound they would easily wipe us out. Ants have a collective mind and we have individual consciences. Our attempts to destroy ants are largely unsuccessful and they may form up to a quarter of the world's terrestrial animal biomass but such estimates are impossible to verify.

Certainly ants are aggressive and versatile like humans: they think nothing of stealing from another group if they judge potential success, are very tribal and even have some parasitic species which don't work, relying on food found by their hosts. Some ants also cattle-farm aphids for honeydew, protect them in return and even farm fungi and also trees they need for making nests by killing surrounding plants. Ants clearly exhibit very intelligent collective behaviour such as teaching skills, despite individually having a pinhead sized brain. They have been around for over 100 million years longer than modern humans (on the inaccurate official timeline), forming better symbiotic relationships with other creatures than us.

Due to high levels of human compliance and stupidity, ants are now the most intelligent species on Earth.

Both ant and human phenomenal success over other life-forms may be down to just evolving arms and legs which are much more useful than claws, fins, wings, etc; expanding the brain to cope with the extra options available and adopting the same trial and error, teaching, cultural genetic and instinctive inheritances we exhibit. It is easy to fall into the trap of anthropomorphising ants and all other creatures to fit into our way of thinking, but ant behaviour is uncannily similar to ours.

Living from a few weeks to 30 years (queens), ants have a much higher reproduction of evolution and empiricism. As multi-trillion superorganisms across the world, ants are debatably as brainy as us. Dolphins are very smart at locating and rounding up fish, but only ants and humans practise farming; no others creatures on the planet do this. Ants also capture and create slave nations too and their super underground colonies are comparatively massive, complex and relentless. Studying ants, we see the same overwhelming fear produced by a species unable to control its expansion or moral code. Ants and humans have two central drives which surmount all: gather as much food as possible without question (money in our case) and produce young to inherit it. Observing the cycle of ants we may predict our own eventual dominating downfall. Humans are just too physically big to take all what we want from Earth without drying out the resources unless we learn to work with nature.

SHEEP PEN PSYCHOLOGY

The matrix is real. Thousands of years of social manipulation and organised coercion have created indoctrination cubes of their own. The NWO want a city and greenbelt divide so they can control you easier and escape their own trap. A lot of critical thinkers experience nausea, panic attacks, IBS (irritable bowel syndrome), migraines, GAD (generalised anxiety disorder) and bouts of unexplained depression with no triggers when they enter or exit the matrix as their minds try to adjust to a change in mental states. Nature is the physical exit door from social control and your intuition is its mental counterpart. Transitional nausea takes place when you are entering a state of relaxation from stress and vice versa or concentrating on something unnatural for too long. To help cope, be relieved you've temporally broken free from drone life and now feeling relaxed, albeit confused. Don't resist the change, let it happen to you. No point trying to achieve much – just go with the flow and sleep more if you have time. Be patient, enjoy things the best you can and it shall pass.

Schools only teach kids how to behave not think. That's why we're in this mess now with so few critical thinkers around.

However the future unfolds, something drastic needs to be done to raise the average person's level of truth and awareness. You've said it a thousand times and will think it another few thousand times, most people are brain-dead and superficial. Accepting this and not getting upset is part of transcending the matrix and breaking the brainwashed free too. When you're smart it's easy to forget what utter morons most people are proving to be. They read nothing of importance, believe their government wouldn't lie about serious topics like health and war, they put their heads in the sand and see truth as an enemy to their overall comfort. Sheeple and governments really don't want us sharing the truth, so keep going and keep the truth alive. Be thankful for anyone who shatters your reality with the truth because they're doing you a favour in the long run. Governments will fuck you over in a heartbeat, friends may unexpectedly let you down, yet feeling good by investing time in the great outdoors is a sure thing. And save your kindness and integrity for people who deserve it.

Once you understand your leaders have been brought up to think of you as vermin it all fits into place.

Following the familiar sunken path that centuries of citizens from all countries and times have trodden, the matrix is designed to be like a magnet for humans, pulling us closer and closer to a locked down, trapped state of mind. Imagine thousands of cardboard boxes glued together with doors cut here and there. Some holes you can crawl through, some boxes need ripping apart and others stop you dead in your tracks. Cycles of corruption are clockwork thoughts within us all, like never really knowing the time in a society full of appointments. It takes either a madman, a suicidal desperado, or a brave thinker to deliberately make themselves lost in order to find the disappointing truth that timelessness is not a human quality.

Is there anyone alive who hasn't had a private reverie on ruling the world to make life better. To seek absolute power is not a natural way of thinking. The matrix is a nasty game, yet a harsh reality the drunk on power oppressors make us play. Privileged people with soft hands yet vicious agendas would see us dying in the gutter if it suited their plans and our seasoned willpower hopefully keeps us from falling. Your unofficial leaders think of you as cattle to cage, so we have to remind them we're not made of wool and it's us who make the world go round. The cult carry out the bidding of supernatural forces they themselves are slave to. Society is a chain-link of lies forged into reality by the fires from hell.

Criminally wealthy people become as lonely as a travelling vagabond. The former buys people, the latter begs for survival. We pity NWO sickos and strive to punish and cure them of their torment: to take so much potential safety and happiness away from less fortunate people must be a miserable, empty existence because we are all just residents renting time and resources from our noble landlady, Mother Nature. The global establishment are such cruel and inhumane people it's enough to wonder if they are people at all or another species putting us down for supremacy.

I've always wanted the world to end and now it's happening I've changed my mind.

Many individuals can be very clever and kind-hearted, but as a pyramid species who would rather choose evil leadership than lead ourselves, humanity has proven to be very stupid and painfully gullible. We cannot feel complete until our minds have ticked humility, patience, uniqueness, character and altruism off our personality bucket list. There's little point achieving anything if it doesn't help someone else as well.

Running round in a mousetrap made by us, humans are our own worst enemy, so no surprise then we begin to betray ourselves and develop mental illness, fatigue and a lack of self worth. It can feel very frustrating being in a game where you never get to roll the dice and if you have a free mind it's hard, maybe pointless being friends with anyone who believes the matrix develops naturally, because at some crossroads they will betray you for telling the truth. Rise above the parapet of our present consciousness and mode of living, and never feel powerless in a faceless society. Stubbornness can come in many veils and friendly guises Adopt a mule's mindset against subjugation. Society definitely needs pig-headed characters who refuse to compromise or be bought for the good of truth and all. Let love and peace exist in our hearts, which in the street becomes understanding, tolerance and self-defence.

The matrix is compacted cruelty, forged by Satan's slaves over countless millennia. That sounds a tad melodramatic but top level evil needs a zero bullshit introduction. The matrix is designed to program you to rarely go outside of your comfort zone or explore every part of your town like you would if you were a hunter-gatherer. House to vehicle to work and back again. The main negative results of confinement is people not questioning things because of seeing the same reality all the time and not talking through social problems face to face. The electronic monetary system is the main network for creating an artificial environment, the legal world its protection and the class system to uphold the rich/poor divide. The split second you are born - even before - you are subjected to hundreds of years of laws specifically designed to defend wealthy people and put you under the cosh. There are literally millions of laws and social rules and regulations, and few have your best interests at heart. The letter of the law is trying to overtake God.

The general idea is to tangle you up in so much red tape and frustrating legislative details that you give up fighting for normality and become like a well-trained police dog jumping through hoops and attacking who you're persuaded to by the State. Mountains of unnecessary rules are created to crush your spirit, control your actions and give the self-appointed elite an escape from prosecution. The legal arena is the antithesis of the human soul. And justice is rarely served either. Technology will be the main future mechanism for social control but for hundreds of years the law has been and still is the bedrock of Satan's palace for the world's wealthiest families to exploit and abuse poor people.

Every time you have any change in lifestyle or join an organisation for education, work, entertainment, etc, the matrix's law is working away in the background, removing your rights and siphoning off your money. By just opening your own tiny one-person business to make a few quid you instantly have multiple government, council and private organisations reducing your bank balance before you've even made a brass farthing of net profit, or you can't legally operate. Simply put, the law regulates your behaviour against your favour and freewill. Inside the core of the matrix is a gigantic pyramid of legal jargon weighing you down so you can't think straight or move without the authority's say-so. Unlimited money printing is the clock of the matrix, the cult of materialism its cogs and medical fascism the pendulum they want you to walk in time with.

In essence, the law is a huge, continuously expanding library of restrictive rules, guarded and enforced by the police and army who are paid handsomely for their level and time of training in comparison to other professions, to ensure loyalty in the face of often justified public adversity. Now that most schools across the world have been turned into private businesses, our greatest fear and real danger slowly coming true is the authorities using a school's compliant and obedient platform to not only indoctrinate your children with biased, brainwashing syllabus, but much worse, exercising legal control and guardianship over your children whilst in the school's attendance. Combined with the forthcoming social scoring system, schools will be the gateway to removing your parental rights using teachers, social services, psychologists, local council, lawyers and the police to prize you away from your own children if you don't obey the State's unnatural and unnecessary rules which basically amounts to doing exactly as you are told, even if this entails euthanizing yourself and your kids with experimental vaccines.

Just a few years ago the aforementioned point would have sounded very tinfoil hat or maybe just crazy, but recently there's been a very sharp rise in the West of low income single mothers losing their children through poverty and now the covid plandemic is setting new legal precedents on child custody which are nothing short of irrational and authoritarian.

Child removal is big business. Each child is worth the cost of a house in fees. In just 2021 alone there are thousands of worldwide examples of routine totalitarian abuse of the family unit using very minor infringements or petty rule breaking as the excuse to separate parents from their children. One pertinent example in 2021 of how absolutely nothing can flare up into a mother's nightmare happened to a family physician, Dr Micheline Epstein, who had her 6 year old child removed from shared custody simply because she didn't wear a mask when dropping her daughter off at school in the open air. Furthermore, the judge ruled she wasn't allowed to remove her daughter from the expensive private school and in the two supervised visits allowed per week, Micheline had to wear a mask in her own home. She also missed her daughter's 6th birthday party. How can any of that be best for the child? Presumably as a doctor, Micheline knew that flimsy masks are ineffectual at preventing the spread of viruses, yet billions of discarded masks do kill countless thousands of creatures. Another American woman called Melanie Joseph was in the middle of a years long custody battle over their teenage son when she posted a selfie not wearing a mask in a dentist's waiting room and was told by the judge she had to have the covid vaccine or she couldn't see her son again. Single mothers seem to the most common victims of this type of unfairness.

Things are going to get much worse before they get better but I have a clear feeling we're eventually going to win and it's all going to be okay. My two pennies worth.

The shocking power and reach of the law into your family life is going to become far more prominent than most people realise. The CDC have already said that in the near future, due to Covid-19, children may need to have a "sudden emergency sleepover" at school. Next very much on the cards, your child could be removed from school without your knowledge, taken to a virus isolation facility and held for a couple of weeks or more without you even knowing where they are or what's happening to them. Looking further down this nightmare scenario and dystopian line of possibility, your child could be sold for the thriving global sex industry and you will be informed they died of covid, and the body was supposedly cremated to cover their tracks. If you think that sounds far-fetched, paranoid or just bloody mental, think again because much verifiable proof exists showing prisoners and care home residents are regularly murdered for private organ donors in numerous countries. And of course in many countries like Venezuela, Colombia, Sri Lanka, Haiti, Thailand, Brazil, Mexico, India, America, Belgium, Canada,

England and China, children are hired-out, abducted or sold all the time for established underground paedophile rings.

It's impossible to calmly explain to a stranger what's going on without sounding like a lunatic because the people calling the shots are lunatics with insane ideas.

In America, under Obama's 8 year term from 2009-17, the administration admitted it could not account for approximately 90,000 children released from the system, thousands given to sexual predator sponsors who forced them into sexual abuse and/or working as child labourers. Barack Obama won the Nobel Peace Prize despite hundreds of innocent children dying in 506 drone strikes he authorized in Pakistan, Yemen and Somalia. Children should never be considered collateral damage. The West is falling and the New World Order are gaining the legal power to remove your children from school and administer medical procedures without your informed consent, against your inalienable rights.

The matrix uses every trick in the book to divide and conquer the family unit, so we must fight with our lives to defend our beautiful children when that dreaded time comes. When confronted with powerful soot black rotten souls, only a united people with the light of righteousness can save the world. Prepare to fight the forces of evil to the very best of your ability with as much cunning as you can muster and to be the warrior you always knew you could be.

This is going to be the biggest war
between good and evil
this beautiful world has ever seen.

TECHNOLOGICAL MATRIX

Once genetic regeneration and robotics keep wealthy people alive much longer than the peasants, we are looking at the future paradigm and carcass of slavery. Humans are not robots, cyborgs, androids, clones, automatons or synthetic representations. We are people with sensitive emotions who struggle to come to terms with a heavily controlled society.

Since computes went mainstream roughly 40 years ago, they've really upset our mental equilibrium much more than appreciated, sucking us into a digital void of unimaginable frustration and fury, and unfortunately they're here to stay. Using computers is bad on your eye to brain connections and bad for the soul. They are an established workplace necessary evil; a contradictory phrase becoming all too frequent to describe everyday life. Computers upset people because there's too much information to take in and no matter how accomplished, the machine always breeds new programs and languages beyond your immediate comprehension. When something goes wrong while using a computer - as it frequently does - we often lose perspective, get wound up, internalise and produce stress. Parents only have to observe a couple of healthy teenagers happily returning home from a park to play computer games until shortly after the frenzied button pressing commences the arguments, aggression and unhappiness bounce pent-up frustration off the walls. If chaos and isolation produce mental illness, then computers are an equally unhelpful tool to replicate negativity. Computers and emotions simply don't mix well because technology gives you tunnel vision and makes us fed-up. They may produce more professional and faster results, but computer usage is also often very time consuming, eating into precious social connections. Some programs can take absolutely ages for you to get completely nowhere unless you're an expert. Computers are a great way to control and isolate people too. I think we would be much better off not using them at all. They produce linear mindsets, are highly addictive and also another gateway to bombarding you with advertising.

Have we really got to a virtual point where we like way more people you've never met on social media than in real life?

Living in a virtual world can be very psychologically damaging and draining. Dealing with code, formats and viruses is an illusion and isn't good for you like something as real as carving away at stone to create a sculpture. Computers are a weird split between fantasy and maths. By searching and pushing for optimum efficiency we are putting ourselves out of a purpose to wake up everyday.

Humans love to use our hands with hammer and stone, thread and needle, thatching, chipping wood, handwriting, using a tennis racket, etc. We have a natural symbiosis with manual dexterity, fresh air, sunlight and face-to-face conversation. Computers save businesses hours but seem to waste individual's hours and they are not a relaxing tool to use. And people are significantly worse communicators since mobiles turned up. The constant interruptions can drive you mental. What happens when all manufacturing is produced by robots and those same handy robots run the house as well and drive you to work. The answer is they won't be driving you anywhere because you won't have a job or anything useful to do. Eventually in our dark future, obsolete people living on State benefits will most likely be euthanized.

David Attenborough promoting 5G is like hearing Mary Poppins sold crack to kids.

In the last 15 years or so, literally hundreds of social media sites have gained enormous popularity and one in particular has debatably changed the course of history. Much more of a covert psychological experiment than about casual chatting and making connections, we have witnessed the organised control of nearly one third of the world's population. Providing free and easy entry into its matrix, on the face of it, it's a welcoming internet environment for friends and family to stay in touch. Underneath the glossy veneer, your personal information is stolen and sold to governments and private companies mainly for sales marketing but also for blackmail purposes of key figures standing in the New World Order's way.

Facebook is the world's largest sheep pen,
a digital metropolis packed
full of small minds.

Beyond the obvious sinister uses of knowing everything about you and mapping everyone's facial recognition, behind the scenes, psychologists, sociologists and computer programmers are studying your data and behaviours to shape an Orwellian future. When billions of people join a huge club of sorts they have to adhere to its censorship style and advertising algorithms or get suspended or banned. Known for blocking all forms of free speech opposing government and world order narratives, we greatly underestimate how much Facecover has helped to shape a politically correct international society of controlled thought.

On Facefuck everyone lies and makes out
their lives are amazing. On Twitter
everyone can't wait to tell
you how shit it's going.

Before smartphones existed, people said what they liked in their own little castles, whereas now they do exactly the same with the entire world listening from the luxury of home without thinking through the consequences because it's easily done. For the first time in history, everyone from around the globe can find out your philosophy, beliefs, political allegiance, inner thoughts, sexual preferences and private desires as if they were inside your mind. All of this delicate and individual information is gathered, analysed and stored in huge databases for the authorities to use at will if you step out of line. Subsequently, many people end up creating an alternative version of themselves, an alter-ego if you like, so their personal lives are left unexamined and un-probed. Everyone is aware they are being monitored by strangers, or local enemies you've made and also by numerous government organisations like the tax man, social services and police forces who have thousands of staff in each country *monitoring* your words and mind. Therefore, without virtually everyone realising it, they slightly change their online behaviour in fear of being caught out saying something not deemed politically correct, socially acceptable, appropriate or safe and that ladies and gentlemen is Big Brother in all its manipulative glory.

Facebook is basically for people who never want to learn a single thing about life.

Consequently, even people who crack causal or stupid jokes after a few drinks can find themselves on the sharp end of a police state. The whole idea is not only to get you to be afraid to speak your mind but to have a well organised international set up in place to rapidly catch out anyone daring to be a real human with normal thoughts who makes small mistakes now and then. No doubt lots of real crime is stopped because of social media too, which obviously is a great thing, such as paedophiles tempting youngsters to meet up. However, all powerful spy tools like Pegasus and enormously popular social media sites are like digital mega-countries of their own that have the frightening potential to lock down whole civilisations and huge pressure groups striving for freedom. In the hands of the New World Order, these electronic super-platforms can be very effectively used to quash small uprisings and silence massive rebellions against tyrannical rule just by identifying and picking-off each person one-by-one. All dissenters, revolutionaries or just concerned and worried citizens are already on massive lists so that dictatorships can suppress and control their opposition by most importantly knowing who they are. Wars were once fought with bullets and bombs, now it's with mass information, fraudulent statistics and medical fascism.

Anyone who volunteered for an experimental jab so they could eat a free pizza, burger or donut wasn't going to make it through natural selection anyway.

Into the deep.

The fall from grace

Madmen want to switch dissenters off by pressing a doomsday button. Lots of us have seen disturbed zoo animals pacing up and down, going out of their minds with a lack of space and mental stimuli. It can be very upsetting watching depressed looking caged animals swaying back and forth trying to cope with their unnatural imprisonment under the guise of valuable scientific research. Humans with little opportunity or hope exhibit similar mental stresses, frustrations, ticks and obsessions. Worse still are poor little rabbits, rats, monkeys, guinea pigs and mice in test laboratories being injected with *god knows what* for the good of mankind. Every living creature seems to be at the mercy of global corporations and this needs overcoming if we are to show the wonderful world of animals how much the people with a heart, care and love life. Nature is your origin, park and place to gather your thoughts.

When you come across a stranger with a can't be bought type integrity it's like finding a £50 note on the ground.

We are so scared at the enormity of the universe inside our minds, the last thing we need is to complicate things by listening to another person's perception of us. At the mercy of the elements in the wild, our behaviour is much less confused than that of the city ape we've become. To protect ourselves from hardship we've created a super complex labyrinth of pretend opportunities and dead ends. Just like in nature, force and fear dictates the order of food and wealth distribution, yet cities are convoluted systems producing much more unfairness, anomalies and abnormal ways. Lots of mental illness results from unnatural confinement, restrictions and a drought of organic stimuli. Madness can be contained, cloaked, sealed and hidden way down so deep that even ourselves don't know there is distress within our minds, but eventually the leaks show and stigma is stamped by gossip. Like it or not, mental illness is a weakness and asking society to ignore their fears and not judge a person's emotional problems is like asking dog owners to pick up their dog's mess when it's dark and nobody is around. It's unrealistic to have a weakness and expect nobody to negatively label you, make fun of it, exploit or steer well clear of your issues.

Half the people admitted into insane asylums probably told the truth too much.

Playing the victim never helps but it's easy to fall into that psychological trap in a duplicitous society that punches out more daily victims than coins. Even if you're determined not to subscribe to a woke and feminist victimhood culture, you'll inevitably be a victim of one of society's main institutions at some point in your life, be it bullying at school, tax office inefficiency, police injustice, medical error, care home neglect, etc. A land of fake opportunity hasn't accidentally grown random, failing and exploitative rotten apple businesses spoiling the core of society. The modern seed, roots and trunk are all rotten, with some good apples making life tolerable and enjoyable. Society is designed to make you ill for profit and depopulation purposes, so if you can rise above this you have strength of adaptability and some greatness in you.

The nauseating sheep will do anything to be accepted, and the minority group of thinkers and prophets value truth above popularity. Sycophants, suck-ups, brown-nosing creeps, mega-weak sheep, bootlicking bombasts and snivelling cowards are always prepared to prostitute and blinker their minds to get on. Many know they don't have the stomach to face bullies and certainly not an austere, establishment system that swats the little people dissenters like flies on their picnic. With this chicken-shit attitude in mind, the obsequious person spends their lifetime grovelling for tit-bit raises and begging for minor rewards to use as show-off currency.

> Free thinkers hear a lot more than
> just what they want to hear.

Alternatively, life's heroes learn it never pays to butter up to The Man because they visualize a shocking future unless more righteous people with balls take a hit for team humanity. There are throat-gulping consequences of having integrity and standing up for what's right, like homelessness or death, yet many decent people would rather suffer misfortune than be a willing contestant in the game of life. Society is a charade and circus laughing at its own performance. When any species gets too big for its boots the sole falls off. We need protected human rights preventing us from becoming victims of global corporations whom for the last 50 odd years have slowly but steadily drained the humanity and kindness out of so many people. Money can make you sick with envy and apathy.

Crazy conspiracy theorists on social media have now become the world centre for truthful information.

It may just be a pipe-dream for now, but in order to call ourselves *civilized* and say we are living in a democratic society we must enforce some basic global living standards and altruistic ideals. Everyone should be entitled to clean running water piped to their home without fluoride or other unnecessary chemicals added. Fresh produce, groceries and meat should be easily affordable, and food wastage significantly lowered. The air and seas should be unpolluted. Corporations producing all the plastic and junk should be made to clean it up. All homes must be free of significant damp problems. Essential industries such as water, food, electricity, gas, etc, should be publicly owned and cheap to use so we're not held to ransom by our basic needs. Everyone should be entitled to a job and be able to get a mortgage under an affordable housing scheme. Any inadequately provided for children should receive the very best of care possible. Homeless people should be guaranteed a bed and meal for the night in sufficiently funded homeless shelters. No organisation should be allowed to own or to have links to more than one brainwashing media centre. Every child should receive a free, high standard education with healthy school dinners and daily fresh milk. Waking up from this utopia, in real life every last government run sector is penny-pinched and deliberately run into the ground until privatisation buys it for a pittance. Humanity commonly betrays itself and every other creature too. Society is trash. There's fuck-all community spirit or friendliness left. We need to dump this rubbish society and start all over again without the mega-wealthy psychos.

> It used to be survival of the fittest,
> now it's survival of the smartest.

There are numerous common and crazy symptoms of the sickness of modern societies, such as loneliness, tiredness and feeling negative, depression and anxiety, madness, suicide, homelessness, prostitution, stalking and even cannibalism. Society has absolutely no qualms kicking anyone to the curb who doesn't comply like a good little boy or girl. Hopefully you can only imagine the nightmare scenario of having to live rough on cold paved streets. The global cabal of elitists use this constant threat and fear of homelessness to ensure most people obey and pay their taxes. A problem with living off-grid, outside of the box is that cardboard isn't waterproof.

LONELINESS

Loneliness has become one of the main side-effects of society. Way more than status or greed, we want a sense of community and belonging. A co-operative community is the heart and hub of your outside happiness. As cities become more populated, oddly people become lonelier. The lack of cohesive local communities, the poor/rich divide, materialism and ever increasing broken families are the root causes of loneliness. And social media is cleaning up on this misfortune, attracting tens of millions of people who have few or no decent and trusted friends outside the electronic matrix. With less and less women choosing to have children too, the serious psychological problem of feeling lonely, in many cases directly leading to suicide, is only going to get considerably worse as scores of wrinkled tattooed elderly people won't have a blood relative to protect and care for them.

A good friend is someone who can finish your sentences for you, but doesn't.

Big society spawns isolation, but you are your own person who can make a happy little world full of love and kindness. Stay upbeat, smile lots, be positive and chatty but not too chatty, always have a good word to say, give out love to the world, join groups and find a hobby or two. Loneliness is a social disease greatly alleviated by generous spirited people.

One of the best feelings in the world is knowing you're not alone.

Extreme loneliness is debilitating. You walk down the street and people feel alien and divorced from you, like you're not allowed into their world. Your heart is crying inside and strangers sense the sadness which puts them off knowing you, furthering the loneliness. You totally lose your confidence and mojo, and your charisma dies with your hopes of ever finding a good friend, let alone a partner. Serendipity cries itself to sleep every night. You're in the same world as everyone else but you feel lesser than a third class citizen, somehow not permitted to take part in the fun and games, even though nobody said so. If someone says hello you're almost taken aback and then embarrassed when they see from your face how far away you really are, you may as well be on bloody Neptune playing the world's smallest violin. After months of having no-one to properly talk to, your mind accepts defeat and depression as the norm, as if you're going to be stuck in that heart-wrenching, melancholic scenario forever, losing all drive and ability to do anything about it. You're so disconnected and lonely you forget that only you can save yourself.

TIREDNESS AND NEGATIVITY

Most of the time that we're consumed by negativity we create many reasons in our head why, but it's mostly because we're physically and mentally drained. Depression is caused by a prolonged state of confused mental fatigue. When feeling down, your mind struggles to pinpoint any particular catalyst so it travels around in pointless circles looking for the bad emotions to blame and sort out, which in itself is draining. Thousands of neurons and many chemicals mix and talk together to form who we are. If we don't provide them adequate rest and fresh fuel, then negativity creeps in and we start to feel frustrated, lost, unhappy, stressed and useless.

A common defensive reaction to mental tiredness and negativity is to defend your bad behaviour in some kind of final proud stand against your unwanted emotions. This is the worst version of you, so you try to fight back and regain the other good and friendly person you were on a different day. Everyone's emotions go up and down all day long. Many people get sugar dips or a flavour of afternoon melancholy. The experienced mind develops prevention, coping and accepting strategies for continuing to perform at work, etc, without upsetting anyone else or themselves. As always, we prevent mental slumps with adequate lifestyle preparation.

Your vibes are more important than your words.

Nobody likes a bad aura and it's your responsibility alone to keep as stable as possible throughout the day for everyone's sake, including yours. Modern mental health practice has a very bad habit of suggesting to patients that their bad behaviour is a result of their illness, not that their illness is a result of their bad behaviour. Ironically, being diagnosed and stamped with the label of mental illness can give patients a good excuse to do nothing to self-correct their unhelpful behaviours and bad habits. Of course, no-one wants to hear that unwelcomed truthful news, especially if they've built a fortress for their negativity to prevent facing life.

When feeling tired, negative and down your options close; ideas shrivel to nothing; a blank mind; you get negative with a capital N; have a go at others for stuff they haven't done; feel absolved from sorting issues out; yawn; dark itchy eyes; unpopular; an aura of a snake creeps in; just want people to leave you alone; go round in mental circles with déjà vu; heavy legs and lethargic; eat rubbish comfort food; you feel lost and useless; need distraction; get a headache, migraine or run-down cold; struggle to focus on anything; and mostly you get low because you feel weak and vulnerable. Most people simply need much more quality rest with plenty of early nights.

When you feel down low,

seek inspiration from up high.

When weary and consumed by negativity, just let things slide, be calm, quiet, happy and avoid confrontation. Forget your ambitious dreams for now and stick to the basics. Act casually, speak less and don't overreact to things. Save your battles for another day. Try not to look vexed as this may invite trouble. Instead, appear to be content and let life's energy flow through you as if you are the lightning rod, not the lightning. Train your subconscious to boost your confidence by positively reminding yourself what you can and have achieved. Stay calm and just keep on effortlessly repeating the mantra, "I feel good" hundreds of times over. Always use positive auto-suggestion to raise your spirits.

Talking yourself up is not genetic, it's an underused lifehack anyone can develop, including you.

> Forget to love yourself and people will steal the love from you.

DEPRESSION AND ANXIETY

Society can drown you in worry and stress to panic stations where your mind and body can't take any more shit. Since the NWO implemented a shock rein of tyranny on innocent people using a fake pandemic as their cover story for taking over, depression and suicide rates have astronomically rocketed as people lose their loved ones, jobs, homes and relationships spiralling into a pit of depression.

Depression feels like a big draining sea sponge moving around your body and head. In a state of extreme anxiety and mental illness, life loses all of its meaning as dark days set in. Your life becomes just about base survival to hang in there and hold on to hope, which is always around the corner. Laughter has sadly gone out the window, so never lose hope because it's your best aide to cure your ills. Hope is the very bottom and beginning of working out a resolution to your multifarious problems. Hope can divorce itself from your state of physical sickness and grow new shoots of optimism desperately needed as a better vision of the future by remembering better days in the past. However, sometimes hope isn't enough and you need to take action to regain sanity. Depression isn't black and white, it's every colour in the world mixed into a muddy grey brown. If you are drowning in depression, then please absorb the following self-help advice:

You have not always been depressed and therefore are not stuck in this pitiful ball of tension forever. Life will get better; you need to believe in that. Right now all you see is darkness and a big wall in front of you everywhere you look and think. Your options seem so limited and one-dimensional they are totally flat and without air. Chances are you've completely painted yourself into a corner by sticking to your guns, knowing in your heart your approach and attitude wasn't the best way forward. Now you're going to have to lose face and some honour asking for help and/or fighting and acting your way back into life. It's OK, we all make loads of mistakes and there's no good in beating yourself up about things you've done wrong in the past because you can't change them. How did it come to this unhappiness, you may ruminate. Forget analysis, the past and the future for now. Instead, exist solely during each section of the day and only reserve a game plan for escaping any torment in non-panicked times. Live in the present.

> You only mentally struggle when you
> don't know what to do about it.

Your twin best friend after hope is belief. You must believe depression and anxiety are not permanent states of oppression you're in. So say to yourself, calmly, determinedly and over-and-over again, "I am going to get myself out of this", "I love myself" or "I love you," as if the words are coming from someone else or a god protecting you. And then take some great advice from *the one and only* Muhammad Ali who said,

"I am the greatest. I said that even before I knew I was."

You need to slowly and surely negotiate a good way out of this jumbled puzzle and convince your powerful mind that a pain free and better life is on its way soon. Begin to love yourself right now because everyone has the potential to be great including you.

You can never find your way without first getting lost.

To begin the recovery process you must help your body out first, which is tired, drained, under strain and searching for answers. The body is sending out continuous, sometimes relentless signals that you're possibly not going to be able to hold-out and sustain the psychological pain and panic without potentially folding-in on yourself. Don't forget, your body is almost always trying to find a solution and does its best to move anxiety around the body to give each section a respite. I understand that being actually sick in a bucket with worry is awful, bloody terrible in fact, but if that's the level you're at or approaching then that's where you shall begin because you have no choice and really want to live a nice life.

Perspective is power. A chained slave hundreds of years ago had to make the best of it with no hope of betterment. We live in relative extreme comfort nowadays so you're lucky in one respect. In the very old days you'd be forgotten and left without care or end up in bedlam. Despite modern social problems, you are in a relatively prosperous social age nowadays. Imagine the past and try to feel grateful that your relative nightmare is in perspective and nothing compared to the extreme horrors in history. This is some consolation because you have a platform to work from now. Dig in deep and feel the animal inside you wanting to live. Awaken that rough untapped strength within you and bring it to bear when you feel at your worst. You are going to have good times and that's what is going to happen! We have heard countless true stories of remarkable survival won by people lost in the wilderness with no food or hope and hardly any water for weeks, and they still made it. Our willpower is separate from the mind and body; it is the outer layer of our soul.

The minute you fear losing, you start losing.

You are going to use common sense to get out of trouble; more reason than surface cognition. When depressed your body is very unhappy, your mind equally fed-up and drained, and possibly all the people around are unhappy with you too, if they're still there (sometimes parents, grandparents or friends feeling obliged to house people, equally clueless how to move positively forward). If you've got anyone genuinely helping you, not exploiting your weakness, show them some sign of appreciation and promise, and deliver a profitable emotional and financial payback when things are better. Your aim is to get well enough to think about their needs and help them when they need it one day. Altruism helps conquer mental illness.

> Don't ruminate on lost love.
> Adore the light of learning.

Maybe a series of unfortunate events has generated a lack of enthusiasm for life, or you made some mistakes you now regret, or perhaps the covid plandemic has driven you into the ground. Whatever has led you down this wrong and mud-crazy track doesn't matter for now. Whose fault it is that you have entered into a mental quagmire is currently unimportant and very unhelpful mulling-over errors you made at some point in your life. Your only task at hand now is to get well again; well enough to make good decisions that influence others productively, instead of being at the mercy of society and negative family. You want to willingly accept as much constructive help as possible. Look for all guide dog and mentor avenues; get yourself a wingman, a top chick, an aide, back-up, reinforcement and treatment to support your move to a better, well-rounded life. Independence is not a good thing if you can't function normally.

The beginning of your recovery has been forced upon you by overwhelmed exhausted senses going ten-to-the-dozen. You may even be termed a Highly Sensitive Person. It matters not whether you accept you're mentally ill because by this stage, fear should've pounced enough to shock you into this uncomfortable, sometimes demeaning realization. Perhaps you've always known there was an underlying weakness and now it's inappropriately erupting of its own free will? Or maybe you're at the dangerous don't care stage? Either way, good options are available and out there; *outside* being the operative word in the sunshine as much as you can. If you feel in any way suicidal, do not mess about or have any shame: call for help immediately! Suicide is never the answer to any problem, no matter how bad or painful. Free help and good advice on mental illness is always available from mental health charities and especially on social media. If you fall into darkness, there will always be someone who can guide you to the light.

If your mental health problem is really uncomfortable, even horrible, yet you've had no suicidal thoughts, you need to rally as much support from as many family members and friends as possible. Do not take your life less seriously than anyone else's. Every last person on this planet has the right to a normal and enjoyable life. Nature provides all the answers for you but that shall take time to absorb and understand. However, just by simply going outside much more regularly and frequently should help a lot.

Unfortunately, much needed humour won't surface unless you return to and balance the basics first; calm (breathing), food, water, movement and light. Learn to counter-balance social negativity and bring dignity and fun back into your life. If you can establish some kind of regular healthy daily pattern, you have a familiar base to build upon. Success has an equal ratio from the bottom to the top, so feel good every time you achieve anything worth having regardless of how small it seems.

Live like you're the bright sun
punching through moody clouds.

Sometimes mentally ill people are known for having a stubborn streak. But when ill and defeated you can introduce the most amounts of reason and ideas that your possible stubbornness and irrationality normally dismisses. If you are moderately or severely mentally ill you have only one option to take if you wish to get better: accept change. The decision to change and get better is ultimately up to you. No real progression will be made until you sit there on your own at home in a comfy place and agree to do what it takes to make yourself healthy again.

Trusting money obsessed psychologists
with your mental health is like trusting a
convicted burglar with your house keys.

MADNESS AND SUICIDE

In your worst times you will likely be consumed with a mix of fear, chronic doubt and lack of hope. This can be very frightening. Nevertheless, if you search deep into your soul, finding and understanding yourself, you'll be surprised how you're not really worried about anything! Fear is often an illusion of erroneous assumptions which hang and claw into everyday palpable thoughts that are always looking to feel fearful when they lose perspective, direction and vision. Irrational thoughts leading to madness are mostly fears of the unknown causing mental chaos. Madness commonly surfaces after drinking alcohol, taking drugs, having extreme repeated panic attacks, experiencing mental exhaustion, or suffering chronic loneliness. These chemical dimensions are gateways to your repressed subconscious which no longer feel the boundaries of conscious displacement activity restraints.

Happiness nowadays is
way too close to survival.

Darkness took a grip on reality and the crescent moon became your only friend. In a mad state of mind, be it a single, continuous action or wild rants, your ability to reason is replaced with random unhelpful ideas and multifarious attempts to search for solace. This always fails because we do not find peace by exploding our energy into hundreds of directions hoping to spear a solid, rational force. You can break the pattern of madness by either echoing the thoughts of a normal person to bring you back to reality, or by continuously asking yourself what you are hoping to achieve with each new search for sanity that pops into your head. Madness is like hundreds of yo-yo's stringing out in every direction imaginable that always bring the worry back to you. A quiet mind is like a sturdy boulder directing a stream which is happy to let the flow of life slowly erode its jagged corners into smooth rounded corners.

If you feel madness arising, or are already caught up in its vortex, you'll likely experience a sense of helplessness, embarrassment or shame for being so lost, mixed with fear, worry, anxiety, anger, frustration, much panic and mostly feeling separated from the world and the people around you. That knotted ball of madness often culminates in a surging feeling of self-righteousness - denying all possibility that you are in the wrong. This happens because madness needs a fixed safe house to recover and recuperate, regardless of righteousness or moral fibre; it just needs to rest somewhere to work out what's going wrong.

> If you want intelligent answers, you have
> to be mature enough to deal with
> the anarchy to your brain.

After being consumed by mad thoughts, the negative and passive aftermath will likely bring feelings of guilt, regret, apologies, possible humiliation, muted anger, excuses and a general concern and knowing that you are not in control of yourself. And people often look to blame either someone else for the result of their actions or their mental illness that made them do what they did. A person's madness may be triggered by others, but you are your own person and must own the responsibility of how you react.

The dark of your loneliness is the only room
with a door to the light of eternal truth.

A mental illness is not the energy and catalyst for offbeat, mad decisions or actions; it is the inherited way you've learnt to organise responses to external stimuli which can be altered with a positive change in behaviour and thoughts, and a general re-orientation of lifestyle and philosophy. Madness is created by the person; it is not the person's uncontrollable fiend who walks in and out of their life regardless of their say-so. If you're in a state of total mental confusion, try and use your common sense to find balance and also ask for help from people who care. Don't try and fight madness all on your own because you will likely lose. Mental chaos can be a terrible shock to your nervous system and knocks your confidence into the ground by leaving you feeling helpless. Please remember to get help through those bad days.

Laugh off every fear and at everything. Crack jokes all day long to yourself and others. Lie to yourself by not taking life too seriously. Go outside, have chats and absorb nature. Care about little nothing. Don't assume anything. Look forward to things instead. Meditate, rest and stay calm as best you can all the time. No arguing with anyone; let things go with the flow. Make, then implement positive decisions throughout your day. Hold onto hope and never despair! Do the right things, then your mind and the world will be with you. Remember your higher purpose in life and always believe you are special.

Unless stopped with prescription drugs, natural remedies and/or expert intervention, madness will eventually snap and break a struggling person's will to live. Very sadly, suicide has risen astronomically during the covid plandemic, made even more tragic knowing the truth. When psychological torment reaches its zenith, the brain feels like a pressure cooker ready to explode and in that tragic state of insanity, you just want out because you can't take it anymore. If everywhere you look there's a presumed brick wall of fuck-all options available, distressing and spidery thoughts of ending your life creep into your mind. Suicide is not the coward's way out, it takes immense courage, but it is *never* the answer. Suicide has to be the saddest of events ever. Someone was gifted a life and they found society so awful they didn't want to live anymore. So many failed suicide victims regret their attempt to end their life and now live happy lives.

Depression is no joke because it fools your mind into thinking there's no hope.

In a frenzied frame of mind, people do the most bizarre things to regain their sanity. One UK hospital in the nineties noted a patient recalling how he actually Sellotaped (Scotch Tape) his left arm to a dining chair at home to stop moving because his panic and suicidal thoughts were so intense he thought he saw another world. He described to nurses a smooth and purple orb, the size of a small red grape with a lustreless surface, floating to the right of him for a minute, which he said felt like a parallel universe revealing itself. In that confused state of mind he could literally see no way forward at all., just a brick wall. This patient's total desperation and pain was made worse by realising he couldn't tape his right arm down because obviously his left arm was already stuck down. Nothing made any sense. He lost his mind and ordered a taxi with the intention of throwing himself off a bridge. Luckily he had no money on him to pay the fare, told the driver and the cabbie refused to drive him so he ended up in hospital instead. The frightening experience was etched in his mind forever, but many years later he enjoyed a happy family life and couldn't believe he was actually going to kill himself once.

When people judge your mental illness
it's like they think you want to suffer.

Society needs more people like that patient to balance out all the boring people but more importantly to remind anyone contemplating suicide that the horror they feel now will definitely not last. There is no shame in having the courage to explore your mind or test your limits. Every explorer needs some help to find their destiny.

Never stop developing your confidence
because the system has a way of crushing it.

Rubbish society.

Transcend the system

The retirement dream is a con, live for now. Society is very disappointing and downright cruel at times, nevertheless here you are making the best of it like you should. There are so many natural wonders to explore and great feelings to experience, it makes you question how we ever lose sight of all the beauty in the world. Life is a great gift so never stop fighting for your dreams and every last breath until your light moves on. Society creates depression and knocks you off track. Nature shows you the true path to happiness. Above all else you must create a worthwhile meaning to your life, preventing mental stagnation and leaving a positive mark on the world. Never ever forget to believe in yourself.

There's a big difference between being open-minded and a gullible twat.

So how do you, hopefully an open-minded critical thinker, navigate yourself around a community full of sheep, lemmings and donkeys because it's not healthy walking down the street expecting people to probably disappoint you. Sociopaths see the hoi polloi as no better than starving seagulls wailing in the wind, yet when you try hard to be a real person with honesty and integrity, the sycophantic sheep will shun you, stab you in the back and choose cowardice over morality every time. In their vast, sometimes overwhelming flocks of stupidity, sheeple are responsible for turning many a good person into a nihilist, cynic, a loner or a loser for not wanting to end up that incredibly brainwashed. When you walk away from trouble, things get less scary but you can lose the source of your identity. A person with integrity doesn't want to clap like a circus seal or roll over like a dog because its master said so. Society simply won't let you be yourself, therefore many clued-up strivers act the part assigned to them and play out a duplicitous lifestyle and mindset, often reaching the hollow fame and fortune they deemed success. And when that doesn't make these social winners happy, they take advantage of and/or abuse people lower down the pecking order, hoping that revenge against the minions will provide new excitement and rewards for their spoils of success in a continuous, almost schizophrenic attack from their self-inflicted misfortune.

An obsession with money will gravitate you into a black hole of negativity. The rest of the awake and intelligent people who want neither to be sheep, sharks or tigers, must eek out some kind of philosophical substance from a rubbish and vacuous society, giving rise to creativity and a deep connection with nature. In the end, our selfishness begins to crave true respect from others, which only comes by being a good person.

The single-minded pursuit of wealth is the deafening instrument of people's nastiness.

If you need to earn money, some level of compromise is inevitable and unavoidable. A strong spirit can transcend the matrix. We are organically free beings who live in emotional chaos. Embracing the truth and meaning of our emotions and unknown origins may be the only force mighty enough to defeat greed. A dependence on money could be termed economic slavery but that's an insult to anyone who is or has been a real slave. Anyway, too much time on your hands and freedom can create mental illness as much as restraint does. A good balance of work and play equals happiness. You're never totally free in any environment and don't want to be either. You first want to find balance then become the fulcrum of other people's balance. Don't become your job, become you. If you've paid a fair amount of taxes, you have every right to ask what your country can do for you, not what you can do for your country. Make sure a misguided sense of duty doesn't sink you.

Don't let your dreams burn out because you were burnt badly or ghosted by society.

At about 25-27 years old, most moderately ambitious people see their high-vaulting aspirations and dreams stop progressing as the social machine chains their energies onto a tax rack and pulls in every limb direction away from their goals and reality. You have your lofty dreams and society simply tells you it's not happening. Others take much longer to resist the symbiosis into mainstream groupthink and some wise fellows never get suckered in, adroitly manoeuvring their way through, under, around, over, disappearing or dodging all attempts to turn them into a compliant drone.

Not fulfilling your dreams and lots of your bucket list is very common, but taking your eye off them foolishly magnetises you closer to a New World Order orphan society. Life dreams are never unrealistic, people's interpretations are. Dreams are there to help you out of yourself and escape the mind warping of demon leaders. Dreams are your compass, your final destination and your spirit of light. A dream has no rank and is heavenly. Walking on our planet is a dream journey in itself, but not completed without planting your own. In your sleep, anything is possible. Beyond the filtering of our anxieties in often boring metaphors, stands your obelisk of destiny amplifying your woken desires. It is a primeval cave in your head, buried so deep nobody can sense its yellow and orange glow but you. Your dreams should be much bigger and more potent than you. Seeing the light only comes from dancing your own flame.

The sheep are guilty of
giving evil a free pass.

Humility is the foundation of higher achievements. There are many unpleasant, degrading and unfair consequences of financial domination, such as going without necessary medical treatment, missing out on great jobs because you didn't go to the right school, or just having to *eat shit* daily from pathetic power crazed management. Adversity and pressure will bring the best out of you even though it may not feel like it at the time, so never give up no matter how low you feel. You need adversity to build up a healthy intolerance of the matrix and the fortitude to defeat evil, so when it's time to rebel, your mind is already on the right page. Psychological capitulation to the money men will cause untold subconscious unhappiness and everyday depression. Don't bootlick anyone or let yourself get whipped, especially by upper-crust morons born with a silver spoon in their mouth. The trust fund babies are mentally weak, cold as ice, jealous and always looking to get one over you. Keep your positivity and pride up all the time. We need to constantly fight back with quiet, determined resistance. Play the system, not people. Mashed potato, fast-food minds have built a zoo to cage our feisty emotions, clocking in and out of every time monitored environment. Don't take your personality out of things because it's what defines you. You are born with a wild tiger's spirit so don't tiptoe around like a pussycat.

> Speak your mind otherwise your enemies will steal your silence.

Jobs are mostly boring, so transform pointless meetings, etc, into potential romances, or customer complaints into good laughs if possible. The psychological damage is done when you feel trapped with no positive options available. Stagnancy creates misery. Try and break up your day with an immobile task, followed by a physical moving task, a thinking task, followed by fun and a walk. Our nomadic origins are most comfortable with an intermittent lifestyle and well-rounded day. Go slowly and calmly with perspective and humour always hovering. You can only complete one task at a time. Thinking jobs over in your mind without doing them only creates mild anxiety and futility. Always have a finishing line set for peace of mind. A successful and happy person is capable of directing themselves without their personality getting in the way of good decision making. Being a good producer and director of yourself will save lots of worry and time. Act like a bigwig trouble-shooter coming from a highflying city into your small town mind, who can clearly see all your good and bad plans, and decisions, then amend them accordingly. Sift out the irrelevant and superfluous to leave golden necessities.

You don't need qualifications to be an expert in anything. Information, experience and knowledge are everyone's to gain.

Don't trap yourself by loving old ways that aren't working. When ideas begin to set in stone they lose their truth. Satisfactory is much better than perfectionism. Perfectionists don't complete things properly. Move around the whole playground. Build a foundation with good preparation before you reach for the sky. Extra projects should be done when you have excess energy, not at the expense of normal living. It is possible to create great things without tearing your mind apart if you pace yourself properly, consistently and appropriately. Make decisions when you are feeling brave, not cowardly, as the courageous thoughts are likely to do good for the world. Be proud that you are facing the system and reality with your head held high. Never feel diminished by your normal life or let a more fortunate individual make you feel lower.

The success ratio of most tasks should be roughly one third doing it, one third organizing and presenting what you have done and the last third convincing others of its success so your efforts are appreciated and get noticed. And when you do a job, do it properly from beginning to end, not in a slap-dash, frustrated way, returning to vex you later. Fix each part well, smooth every corner with pride, organize with skill, clean up after and then stand back and pat yourself on that back for doing a job thoroughly, conscientiously and proficiently. Then have a rest, some fun and on to the next stumbling block in life.

Nothing ever goes perfectly to plan. Life is always about how you react to the changes.

Sometimes you just need to get your finger out and get on with it, rather than wallowing in the problems until muddy and confused. Prioritize well beforehand. Most importantly, don't be workshy or ignore the boring stuff that needs doing, or fall into chaos through laziness or disorganisation. Avoidance of mundane reality creates a sense of hiding and fear like you are prey. That cringing, overloaded and overwhelmed feeling will stay constantly in your mind and start to bury you if you don't show some keenness about you. The kitchen is a mess, dishes need doing, children need attending, the oven could use a clean, must to respond to that insurance letter, running out of milk, respond or not to an old flame, decorating, sort out photos, stop a bully fucking you off, go to dentist, remember to get the small screw bulb for lamp, sort out website, fix wobbly chairs, buy computer security, put family photo on wall, get washing out, check bank account, vacuum, water plants and then meditate with the remaining 2 seconds left. Step by step you will cut every problem down to size and use your experience or someone else's knowledge to deal with every last thing bugging your brain until all you hear is the crisp sound of confidence and capability. And try not to be so conscientious. Let things slide. You can't save the world.

It's time to make the most of what you've got and stop exploring new lands as the answer to problems.

Your days may go up-and-down, yet try hard to keep constantly relaxed throughout. Read what's going on and predict the best time to stop whatever you're doing. Nothing is ever as important as you think it is. Rushing shows a lack of control and planning. The mountain climber finds one good hold at a time and secures themselves along the way. Lots of mini surges of energy throughout the day will encircle and defeat your daily problems much more productively than one monumental push, followed by a lack of enthusiasm. There must be a good general approach to life, seeing the bigger picture and having an *in control* feeling which overlooks and radiates through everything you do.

Your reset position and permanent state of existing should always be one of total calm. This comes first before anything else. Relax and centre your mind whenever you get lost. Being chilled makes you approachable, attractive and fun.

Once you have divorced your mind from society's wishes by developing true character, much wisdom and personal interests, fulfilment will come from having removed your socially constraining shell and stepping into your own skin for the first time. The world starts, ends and carries on with or without you. Life's too short to live in turmoil. Seek peace and holiness. Flow with changes better by seeing your day as a river of thoughts, not a puzzle of tasks.

It's so important to be eager about starting the next day. Without life direction we become lost lambs. Most people appreciate yet underestimate the vital importance of knowing where you're going. Not having a happy and true arrow direction in life is soul-destroying. Being stuck in a rut causes canker, mental illness and even crime. That moment when you finally find your way feels sensational, where perspective is gained, problems are put in their place and all obstacles seem easier to overcome. The essential self-discovery that your purpose in life is paramount, emphasises how perspective and mental illness are primarily introverted problems, literally *all in the mind*, albeit with palpable suffering. When you gain a real purpose close to your heart, many issues feel petty and even insignificant, or at least mostly manageable. Purpose is something to focus on, achieve and look forward to accomplishing. Ambition is the level of purpose.

If you become your own work of art, you will always fail in reaching a higher purpose.

Imagine you're in a baron desert, desperate for water. If you knew for sure where some water was on a map, you could walk about five times more distance to make it there than if you were aimlessly walking into the abyss hoping to find some water. Knowledge becomes energy. Knowing where you're going may be the most important factor in achieving emotional success, otherwise mirage after fantasy will ruin your life as clouds of delusion stop you from seeing the clear sky of reason. The bigger picture dwarfs and overshadows seemingly small problems. Humans need to know exactly what to do and where to be, and often want their hand held along the way. We seek hope, then wise guidance.

Truth doesn't hurt, it's the lies that weren't clever enough to outsmart you.

Existing for too long in mental limbo will strangle your ambition and willpower. Mentally ill people always seem to make a big deal out of everything because everything *is* a hassle when you can't cope and their ability to flow over and around obstacles is often terrible. If you have nowhere to go it's easy to get distracted and create problems that don't exist. Just as bad is not believing in what you're doing because all your efforts are likely to come up empty-handed and an underlying worthlessness slowly consumes you. Finding yourself and knowing how to orchestrate your ideas and energy, allows you to see right through every lie, scam and trap society has waiting for you. Transcendence isn't about being above people, it's about being above yourself using the natural flow of life.

Entwined with financial vines, badgered by irrelevances, knocked by disappointments while having to dig out a meagre to moderate living, yet still your decisions, temperament and presence remain decently constant, then you are touching on higher plains. Enlightenment grows fresh green leaves and sees the real potential in everything and everyone. Your heart's knowledge is the heartwood of your tree. You'll move towards enlightenment by stepping out of the shadows of your parent's influence.

Three personal qualities usually come to the fore with detached minds: they have a higher purpose, simplify their world and follow their heart's knowledge. They also let people be themselves and are equally unaffected by other's negative actions. Problems seem inanimate and impersonal. The enlightened soul continuously exudes humour, a positive, upbeat and calm attitude to life, and obeys moral codes. Enlightenment massages the soul and slows down your pace of life. It is clear that great mental relief and uniformity of our souls is rewarded by becoming allied with all elements of what we perceive as uncorrupted nature and worlds beyond ours. There is a working pattern and rhythm in life which is eternal.

Measure your greatness not by how many souls you have echoed, but by how many echoes you have silenced. Enlightenment is not charisma which pulls us in, rather emotional gravity that keeps you grounded. In a nutshell, enlightenment is accrued wisdom applied usefully and morally. You can't really be taught enlightenment. It's something you work out on your own. Common descriptions by enlightened people are feeling a few metres away from your own body - like it's not you being there - and also as if one's cranium hinges upwards and lets out all the bad stuff whilst simultaneously pouring light in. You'll know it when the epiphany comes. When enlightened you will feel and see people drawn to you and being reasonable.

We know nothing about each other but our souls seem to know everything.

Experiencing the blessing of transcendence can feel like you are surmounting the truth, however, truth *is* transcendent and your connection to pure reality elevates you above corporeal facts to a spiritual dimension where you desire nothing and are happy just hearing your own breathing and thoughts. Spiritual enlightenment is the zenith of apathy because when a supreme feeling of bliss radiates throughout your being, you really, genuinely don't give a fuck about anything. You feel unattached and unconcerned in a great way, like nothing needs sorting out. Bliss occurs when everything makes sense and you remove yourself from artificial concepts and superficial friends. Good feelings are like garden fairies that only come to light when you open up your mind and explore the world with creative eyes.

The experienced and enlightened mind separates then solves their own problems before seeking to confront the evil in society harming innocent people and nature, particularly children and animals. There's not much point being enlightened if you're just going to sit in a temple praying like a reclusive monk when you have the power to improve your community by destroying evil. Courage in the face of adversity is a crystal clear sign of enlightenment, as well as kindness when no-one is being kind to you. Accept that evil powers will always commit murder and genocide because they are maniacal control freaks, therefore your mission is to show resourcefulness and bravery by stopping them dead in their tracks.

Covid is the fake distraction from something so dark it swallows black holes for breakfast.

There's no pontification in a transcendental mind. It knows exactly what to do and where it's going without pause and with *action* being the operative word. He or she standing in the light of truth accepts any outcome destiny has in store. Enlightened people are often loners who never feel lonely, totally happy with their own company and space. They reject the sheep because sheeple are dulled witted and drag society down. You can pass from life to death in a single second, so why ruminate on the fear of momentary darkness when there are millions of moments of light to enjoy. Enlightenment doesn't meditate on a mountain, it *is* the mountain which downpours waterfalls into rivers of wisdom through the thick of it down below.

Hope

Salvation.

Change your nemesis

You want to be monumental, not mental. The whole idea of studying human history and analysing your own personal past is to learn from the mistakes to improve the future. If people can surmount their individual weaknesses, then humankind has the potential to do likewise. Every century we see new nasty faces representing old evil designs which could demoralizingly be deemed the human condition. Nothing seems to ever change other than technological advancements. The New World Order dreamers are always a few steps ahead of technological advancements. None of their AI robots work as planned, the genetic modification science has failed and their space programs are utterly ridiculous. In reality, they can't even make a driverless car without it crashing. And what qualifies as outer space is getting embarrassingly lower and lower. Soon in the passenger space race comedy of errors, roofers will be have to be categorised as astronauts.

> The most important thing to realise in these dark times is you're not alone.

The potential for a higher human awakening by rejecting materialism is there, yet nearly everyone underestimates their personal power to change the bigger picture because history is a long scroll of repeating wars, tragedies and miscarriages of justice. Fear and powerlessness fill the hearts of billions of acquiescent clones of Machiavellian governmental policies. Fear is something that occurs when you are not at one with yourself. There is actually no need to be afraid of anything. You can walk into the unknown if your world is true. Truth conquers all.

The human species is very pessimistic about our ability to produce enlightened minds because society crushes people's spirits and only gives those who tow the line a wider platform to excel. Closed doors to opportunity, social class stumbling blocks, a lack of money and work tiredness culminate in the sad acceptance of failure as routine for many people. Life can really get you down and that's not by accident. The calculated Illuminati plan is to get you to know your place as a slave to their system which only benefits about 1% of the world's population. Having psychos at the top always trying to murder everyone does wonders for one's self-awareness and sharpens the mind, so much so we should almost be grateful. Recently, perspective of life has changed so enormously I wouldn't be altogether surprised if the sun was a light bulb on a timer in a serial killer's basement. He or she who controls their mind is never at the mercy of tyranny. If you fight hard and smart enough you'll always be capable of transcending this evil matrix.

One good way humanity can transcend it's debilitating, collective mental weaknesses is by developing a feeling of pure personal freedom and unrestricted self-belief. And this enlightened revolution of the mind can only happen when you personally decide to make positive changes to your way of life and mindset, regardless of what others choose to do, which goes against the grain of the mainstream media, evil voice of doom narratives. Just one brave person can be the catalyst for a successful revolution against obscene levels of greed and evil when the rest of us divorce our minds from this manipulative, narcissistic paradigm. Sometimes it feels like you're the only person around who faces the truth without suffering stress or mental illness because you understand history which is littered with gross injustices and heinous lies that start war after war. We've been here many times before.

> You can't forgive what you
> don't understand.

Throughout this study of human behaviour, we have identified the fear of death, a delusional lack of willingness to accept truth and reality, a lust for greed, and an obsession with status as the four evil horses trampling the world with sin, preventing our species from psychologically progressing. In addition, the fear of change saddles each and every one of those demons as the top predator of and slayer of human courage and positive evolvement. Behind all failure is somebody who was too afraid to change their routine and set ways. A big hug and pat on the back to any sheep who admit they've been brainwashed by their government and media. It takes character to admit you were duped.

> If you ever wonder if you're stupid,
> you're not.

Most humans absolutely hate changing anything but also believe they're not the one afraid of change until they lose their job and the fear of running out of money, interviews and meeting new people sets in. Financial and mainly psychological comfort surmounts the truth almost any day with virtually everyone. Many people are so set in their ways they have to take themselves out of their comfort zone at least once a month to prevent stagnating in depressive thoughts and stale customs. All human beings were once super-fit nomads and some fearless adventurers, but now most of us like to hide in our little cubbyhole and travel through social media instead, bravely fighting off keyboard warriors behind the safety of a touchscreen. Most people's routines are so staid, rigid and frighteningly similar day after day, that package holidays become a *must* to escape such self-inflicted drudgery. In fact, holidays are pretty much all some people ever daydream about, rather than reshaping a new way of thinking which squeezes the most zest from life.

Search the depths of your soul,

not your cereal bowl.

Where has all the spunk gone you ask. Where's the fight and real men in armour who battle dragons to win the hand of a fair maiden. We live in a dishwasher cycle and bum-wiped society where there's a product to solve every insignificant problem we can't be fucked to solve. Somehow, like a weird bit of media voodoo, most people don't change anything because inside their fragile egos they've been led to believe that small efforts and a mini resistance against avarice and the forces of evil are futile. Not so by any means. *Little strokes fell great oaks, Rome wasn't built in a day, the journey of 1000 miles begins with a single step* and many other truthful sayings and clichés arising from experience show you how important every last aware person becomes if we want a better life for our children.

Even the most ardent pacifist becomes a hurricane when defending their child.

For every 33 clueless sheep buying into our bullshit system, one awake resistance member's good efforts to bring about change is cancelled out. Parental imprinting is such a strong force of nature, once for good survival reasons, that unfortunately our minds are programmed to respect our elders and go with the popular grain of accepted lifestyle routines, be they good or bad for us and thus social betterment means defying the norm. A person not doing what the crowd does nowadays is as rare as tea cosies.

CHANGE OF LIFESTYLE

You can't stop *change* banging on your front door so you must decide if you're going to ignore the cold calling knocks of newness every day, or positively deal with unwelcomed changes. Pleasantly different and unfamiliar nice surprises can be exciting, but too much unknown equates fear (neophobia), psychological retreat and bedwetting. The longer you walk backwards by lingering in the past, the more your future steps for change will struggle to find a good footing. Every day you spend lamenting your lifestyle losses you are potentially building a castle around grief, preventing freedom of thought and also increasing your stress hormones which can lead to severe depression if it goes on for longer than a few months. Drastic unwanted change limits your ability to imagine better options to escape that trapped feeling being overwhelmed produces. You must remember there is always hope and a fresh perspective to show you the light. Whether you have money troubles, a big dip in your emotional well-being, or other significant stresses, there is always a solution to your problems. Worrying is fruitless and gets you nowhere.

Evil wins if you lose
your sense of humour which
is the very essence of who you are.

Make sure you integrate in-and-out of events whilst staying the same person throughout. Flow effortlessly from one job to another task, onto a planned event and so on in a psychologically smooth fashion. Find time for yourself before rushing into more change with a misguided hope that one new situation may be the same as the one you've lost. Try one new thing once a week. Keep your pride up and accept your new situation and fate. You may not like your new circumstances, but they are here and change is inevitable so you may as well welcome a brand new start and look at your new life with optimism. With some courage and determination you can build something great from what you have right now.

GRASSROOTS OF CHANGE

Perhaps misfortune, super stress, being truly sick-and-tired of being depressed every day, or even feeling like you don't belong anywhere has led you to the realisation that you have to change major parts of your approach to life and/or your behaviour. Maybe you've totally had enough of pathological media and serial government lying, or have specifically lost all patience and tolerance with the covid scamdemic. One way or another your instincts or life are taking over and telling you to change. Bruce Lee clarifies,

"Empty your mind, be formless. Shapeless, like water. If you put water into a cup, it becomes the cup. You put water into a bottle and it becomes the bottle. You put it in a teapot, it becomes the teapot. Now, water can flow or it can crash. Be water my friend."

Now you have decided to change, which is *the* most important first step to take, you'll need to gain knowledge of which direction best to take, accompanied by the motivation to implement your transformation. Changing your basic routine is never easy, which is why so many people allow life to overwhelm them before being forced to make different lifestyle choices. Change is good though because it gets you to re-examine negative aspects of your life holding you back and also reinforces the worth of good points and successful parts of your life. To be mentally healthy, you need a small amount of continuous flowing development and newness to your character and life on a regular basis to prevent mental stagnation, and no more than about one fifth expansion and change to keep a steady balance. Nothing will ever stop people from wanting to travel the world on endless holidays and excursions. Travelling, alcohol consumption and eating chocolate seem to have become non-negotiable favourite ways to escape mundane lifestyles. Being creative is better though. It's basically internal travelling and an expansion of the mind's inner world and abilities, and costs virtually nothing but time. In adulthood, we do not lose our childhood creativity. Instead, society actively discourages and suppresses self-expression and freedom of thought. Being creative is one of the best ways to escape anxiety, explore your emotions and gain knowledge of the world and yourself. Everyone is creative.

With art you need no friends
and can survive happily without them.

Face reality by making instinctual decisions about how to solve your problems with a sense of urgency as if you were hungry and hunting in survival mode, or against some harsh stormy weather and need to find a place to shelter immediately. We've got so used to the ludicrous levels of luxury in our previously super-safe society that the sense of entitlement to a basic standard of living can corrupt our natural sense of reality. Look to the future and focus on the present by building a survival strategy. Living in the wild doesn't allow hardly any time for mental reflection, remorse, guilt or even grief. Philosophising is frequently a dead duck.

You won't make good changes to your personality if your mind is locked into or constantly floating in and out of the past. Only your perspective of the past can change, so change that. Get into shape too. Being physically fit and up for it will increase your confidence, your range for positive change and also make you value yourself more. Communicate better as well if that's not your forte. Most people before their thirties, greatly underestimate the importance of likeability factor in relation to success. Whilst striving for status it's easy to lose yourself. No-one really cares what qualifications you've got or whether you've been vaccinated, they want you to show them who *you are* with confidence, spirit and honesty.

> At some point, the fear of viruses will be totally irrelevant to everyone as we are all forced to fight for survival.

MAKING PRACTICAL CHANGES

Nobody likes change. It takes effort to change. Everybody's life seems busy. People don't listen and only want advice when they ask for it. Society dictates only one way. To counter our modern dislike of change, you have to make a conscious effort to put your toe into the water of new stimuli and situations when you feel at your most confident, until there's little fear just diving into the unknown. Step by step you will get where you want to go if your desire to change is strong enough, particularly if you're not happy or dislike who you've become. The last thing you feel like doing when you need to change your negative, broken record ways is to invest energy you feel like you haven't got by changing. This seems counter intuitive and all-round problematic. What is really stopping you though is not lethargy but a fear of the unknown. Fear is the greatest obstacle to change. Fear sticks people's minds in the dunce's corner with a stubborn refusal to shift their thinking. Fear is powerful because it's instinctual and can overwhelm the good within you. Darkness comes in many forms and one of the most successful disguises for evil and fear is self-righteousness. Beware those mock holier than thou fakes who can't wait to jump on some righteous bandwagon to hide their sins or cowardice. Fear is your government's tool for control. Fearless people think alone.

Fear is the food of Satan he devours daily then washes it down with a goblet of people's tears.

Negativity leads people into tiredness and then the stubborn mule inside would rather dig its hooves in and receive a whipping than move a heavy emotional weight. Change only comes most commonly when someone is desperate with their suffering and has no choice but to seek help, or when you are smart enough to predict the upcoming problem and pre-empt failure. You always have more energy than you feel you have once you gain a positive and passionate direction. You have every right and opportunity in the world to live a happy and moderately stress free life. You owe that to yourself to make that happen. All personal mental traps can be escaped. It's just a question of knowledge and willpower. Life is supposed to be simple, fluid and frequently enjoyable. You don't have to live in the shadow of anyone's negative influence dragging you back from positive changes. Have courage to dump negative people because it will pay off in the long run. Admittedly, it does take a spark of energy to re-orientate and motivate your mind into changing, but nowhere near as much energy as stolen by rigid and negative habits. Changing your personality and habits is more about adopting a *do it now, not tomorrow* mentally than waiting for inspiration.

The truth is we are either too tired, being lazy, don't know what to do, or haven't prioritized tasks well enough to enact change and people also don't appreciate the worth of self-learning enough. When you think you are way too busy and knackered to change what you want to change, it really means you're procrastinating. Change best happens right now in the moment you think about changing. Making an appointment to change a personality flaw at a later date is bound to fail. *There's no time like the present* as they say. You're never 100% ready for anything, but you can feel totally prepared. When you start positively changing, you'll build momentum, inspire others too and also double your charisma if you believe in yourself. To fully improve yourself you must accept and embrace positive constructive criticism. If you refuse to take any personal critique then you are not ready for change and will likely stay as you are. Honesty from others or yourself concerning your faults is excellent information about how to grow as a person, so take any negativity on the chin for your own good. This will build character and a strong defence against bullies.

It's amazing how quickly many people can fall apart at the seams if their circumstances change. We are incredibly mentally fragile and consequently employ a vast array of pretences and pretentions to mask our frailness to the point where we ourselves can't see it or just lie. Humans are a veil of a wisp of an idea. We are nature's escaped convicts running riot. Accepting and dealing with the situation you are in, telling the truth and the way you feel is far more productive than pretending it's not happening or has happened. First, a cycle of balance must be found and agreed upon and then that comfortable confidence can learn how to resist society's obscure and evil demands. Reality is where you stand now and the quality of thoughts you fill the air with. Make sure you really enjoy every quiet before a storm and always connect with nature. And keep sharing the truth because millions of lost people need to hear you.

The sheep once mocked people saying The Great Reset was just another stupid conspiracy theory and now they advertise it in shopping malls and on the telly. There's no global warming, no Covid-19 virus and no election winner in the White House. You are in a covert war against falsified statistics stealing reality from you. Thousands of shills pretending to be independent accounts on social media, pushing party lines and global narratives, is a desperate and clear mark of an evil agenda taking over. All soulful and spiritual people can sense a serious Nazi and Stasi style oppression ominously marching this way and many of these clued-up people are starting to crack. You can feel it in the atmosphere. It's your intuition telling you darkness is coming in the form of slavery. That's all the more reason to enjoy life right now and prepare to resist punishment for believing in the truth. Long live the truth!

Don't let fear rule you and get yourself a wingman or bestie to share the burden of awareness. Use oncoming tyranny to sharpen your mind and senses, and strengthen your resolve. Nasty worldwide social changes are upon you, so get used to that factual change *immediately* by positively adapting every day. What's coming will be the biggest change and challenge to your routine, lifestyle and mind you've ever faced. Are you going to sink and let the bastards win, or stay afloat and punish them for their sins?

Never ask yourself when feeling melancholy why it's your turn to fight tyranny, just fight it. My granddad was a decorated WWII navigator in a Lancaster bomber, flying 998 operational hours. He and millions of other brave people fought the same tyranny so the West could enjoy relative peace for 75 years. Once more we must take up the mantle against the destroyers of democracy and kindness so new generations can have a good taste of freedom like lots of us have. We will eventually put an end to this globalist tyranny and we'll be happy about it. We don't want the old normal back. We want to see those responsible for crimes against humanity brought to justice before we start a war on corruption so our children can be free.

Balancing your brain.

The art of calm

You can't defeat evil by being nice or feeling sorry for it.
There is much hope for humanity. Believing we are doomed
assumes you can predict the future. The vast majority of
humans are good people, so if we could raise the overall
level of consciousness to create a higher destiny then
humanity may very well defeat its ancient demons. For
every nemesis there is a solution and saviour. Good always
slightly outweighs evil. Beating the global bullies' lies and
coercion is paramount to success. To win out and move
forward as a species, humans must connect with three core
values. Firstly, practice and increase your happiness quotient.
Secondly, respect the truth, growing pure personal freedom
and unrestricted self-belief. The truth is not a matter of
opinion, it's undeniable fact. Thirdly, develop your intuition,
listen to your heart's knowledge and be open to
enlightenment. And nature's wisdom should run throughout
all parts of your life.

You could spend a lifetime beachcombing
and roaming, yet still never discover
a greater lover and highs than
all the beautiful skies.

Book 2 in my Human Mind Series explores happiness via
intuition and the truth in greater depth, and book 3 covers
everything about bullying, therefore we shall conclude this

examination of the human mind with what I regard as the most important element of hope for humanity positively changing, which is learning the way of calm and practicing meditation, both detaching you from negative thoughts and society's devious blueprint.

Being calm is a cohesive aspect of all the three aforementioned awakening mind mechanisms of happiness, truth and intuition, which can be achieved by every human alive with no room for excuses. It's totally amazing that such a basic thing as being calm could readily transform the world. Unelected leaders get what they want by scaring everyone on a daily basis with fake news and building ministries of lies, simply because they were badly scared and abused as children and weren't emotionally smart enough as adults to find closure and a better way.

Feel your heart being calm and beating slow
as moon tide ripples ebb and flow to
the pulse of your contentment.

Low-level fear-mongering never stops and is only interrupted by frequent made-up national and global emergencies to top up the fear factor: don't eat that or you'll suffer, put your money here or you'll lose everything, stand in that circle and put a mask on or you'll die, and the list of insulting government instructions for life go on *ad infinitum*. The nasty trick is to make you feel like you'll lose out badly if you don't obey every fucking stupid rule and meaningless regulation harassing you. Happiness right now is not obeying, caring or even knowing what the rules are. The simple plan from day one has been to remove your rights, then build your hopes of freedom up again, then hit you with something worse, all to demoralise you and make you lose hope. Just ignore them completely and resist when the time comes. The only build back better we need is a financial revolution. And all of this planned global madness post WWII would be ignored and resolved fairly rapidly if the masses stopped running around like headless chickens and gathered their senses together by simply being calm, not reactionary and ignoring unreasonable demands.

Our social matrix deliberately stresses you out so you can't think straight. If you practice meditation or by chance feel really relaxed you see right through people's lies and won't even dignify government propaganda. Calm is your best defence against manipulation and tyranny. For a start, when you're completely calm you won't fear death or negotiate with blackmailers. You'll also maintain a high level of self-respect and energy which stops you getting abused, taken advantage of, or tolerating being cheated on. Something unexplainable, yet really special and transcendental occurs when you're genuinely calm which ticks off tricky problems one by one with consummate ease and has a latent power no-one messes with.

As you walk across green fields your tired
footstep troubles sink into lush grass until
a spring in your step bounces new
pace and purpose into your life.

Almost every single problem is solved by being calm. You must try to stay calm all of the time. No shouting, no aggression, no panicking, no despair, no arguments, no tension, no agenda - adopting a peaceful state of mind. Keeping a clam mindset is the passkey to see through New World Order deception and detaching from personal struggles. To change the world you need to be able to improve and control yourself first. The way of calm is not just a procedure, it's the first step to understanding how selflessness means an effortless life, not a sacrificial one.

There are two ways you can do things; tense or calm. Calm is much better. Many sufferers of mental illness, social anxiety and/or depression come to believe that positive thinking is of primary importance to their recovery because inexperienced well-wishers advise them to be positive and you'll get through it. Positive thinking alone, without action or awareness, is not as useful as we'd hope in countering the unpleasantness of moderate mental illness and is surprisingly ineffectual to counter severe mental illness because that depth of bleakness isn't cured by shining a small torch of hope for a few seconds into a huge cavern of dark unhappiness, even though it helps a bit and many bits can become whole if you're a surprisingly determined character who lost their way. Socially promoted *fake* positivity - more posing and showboating - is also a good way for sly governments to create more tolerance for the oppressive culture they want. Essentially, positivity comes from your history of happiness, not other people's opinions.

Learning the art of calm is the only simple and timeless technique and philosophy which has a great impact on everybody, especially mental health sufferers, brainwashed sheep and disillusioned streets of anxiety, without needing any supreme knowledge or having to take a pill. Slowly learning how to rethink and reorientate negative habits usually takes months of ineffectual, costly therapy and slipping back into bad old ways later down the line is likely. Yet being calm can be learnt in less than one hour and has proven to have immediate beneficial effects for people drained by mental health problems; particularly overthinking, obsessional disorders, stress and social phobias. Anyone trying to be calm somehow feels much better even if they just fake being calm without knowing anything about how to achieve a deep calm of the mind, body and soul.

Before meditation, which is a different avenue into achieving calm, becoming calm is the number one, most important philosophy for everyone to learn. Ill or not, everybody benefits from a panacea of calm people around. People often talk of complex, seemingly high-minded and unattainable ideas which only people with a lot of spare time can master; Zen this, mindfulness that, seeking eternal bliss, etc. They're great, but just simply being calm is the foundation of all of the hundreds of worldwide philosophies and meditations out there, past and present. A state of pure calm is the mountain peak and triumphantly waving flag of supreme psychology!

BENEFITS OF CALM

There are no down sides to being calm, none whatsoever. Being calm is an essential state of mind to strive for all day long in everything you do and it's also not terribly difficult to enter into either. When you're isolated from the group you panic. Calm solves this. Calm is your thoughts being slower than your heartbeat. Remaining calm in all circumstance is the real trick. People just simply forget how important being calm is. Projecting a calm aura can even stop someone who was going to attack you from doing so. The incredible top 10 benefits of being calm are far reaching and welcomed everywhere they travel:

1. Other people will always like you when you're calm. In fact, it's very hard to dislike anyone in person who consistently exudes calm even if your personalities clash.

2. Unforeseen good opportunities seem to just pop out of nowhere when you're calm and the antithesis happens when at your wit's end facing a brick wall of unimaginative avenues. A calm mindset unravels problems like a magician pulling a knot out of a rope in a second.

3. A constantly calm demeanour can dramatically improve or even cure serious illnesses, frequently caused by stress; particularly the asthma and eczema family, and heart problems. Calm also very effectively stops migraines and headaches developing; it strengthens your immune system to fight off common colds and flus; improves blood pressure and digestion; and the full list of further medical and mental health benefits is impressive. Think of calm behaviour as medicine for your soul and energy for your ambitions.

4. Calm makes you sound confident and clear, and you'll appear much more attractive when projecting a controlled aura. This quiet, confident quality makes you a better lover and parent, and will stop you ever getting bullied because people will sense your reserves of energy.

5. You are much more likely to make honest and rational decisions when calm, and also you'll share your love and enthusiasm for life with others.

6. A calm mind really helps you see the landscape of the day ahead to ward off any potential problems. Being so connected to yourself will make prioritising jobs and filtering out irrelevant and insignificant troubles much, much easier. A super calm mind can give you prophetic vision. You'll likely make more money when you're calm too. Most top businesspersons are well-known for remaining calm under pressure. Calm turns worry, uncertainty, anxiety and panic into manageable and solvable problems, and keeps the truth in its original form.

7. When feeling the equal passivity and strength of calm ways, you can hear your inner subconscious thoughts and find out what you want from life at a deeper psychological level. Calm is the gateway to accessing the ancestral higher philosophies in our genetic memories and also a portal opening our hearts to enlightenment and God. You can't be enlightened unless you are always calm for at least a few months every day, all day – including in your sleep.

8. Calmness also gives you a great sense of humour - seeing the funny side in everything - which can only be good for you and others to keep spirits up. Laughing off trouble works.

9. We connect very well with nature when calm which helps expand your mind to see the possibility of multiple dimensions and provides a natural opening to self-improvement and awareness. Petals are so delicate they're like a lost moment in time where a tranquil mind can live a lifetime of opening thoughts.

10. The most important aspect of mastering the way of calm is its natural rejection of materialism. Love does the same thing better of course, yet doesn't posses the same reliability and stability of a calm mind. If everyone in the world was very calm, money obsessions would die out and the planet could recover. If you can achieve a placid calm mindset, then all sorts of greed (money striving, extra sexual partners, a pricey car, etc) fades away into thinking about positive and creative enterprises instead. To be more precise, when you are really calm you don't *think*, you just do. Being very calm is like experiencing life in slow motion as you watch others frantically rush around like lemmings on acid.

Keep a calm mind and you become a formidable opponent.

Everyone has a rough idea how to simulate being calm because that's our favourite emotional state to be in. Evolution has developed a calm mentality as a supreme crowd pleaser, the dominant behaviour of winners - being the most successful path you could choose. A calm person is always given a voice and is a great hunter and protector too. The greater good has been kidnapped by nefarious forces giving false hope. Staying calm efficiently directs your energy against those forces of evil.

Flow, listen, understand, talk, enjoy.

Let people be, so you be free,

play the flute, be calm and fun,

water, tree, sun, one by one.

Maintaining a state of calm is fundamental to your soul, your general well-being, the world paradigm and to help your family as well. People have always worked their socks off under much more austere conditions and valued calm and comedy as the forerunners to personal success. Stress has not increased, but changed format instead. Contemporary humans have lost the calm connection - held in reverence for thousands of years - because stresses have dramatically changed in nature since the Industrial Revolution and much further again since the development of computers. Also, a genuine commitment to religion has significantly waned in modern times and deep prayer promotes calm thoughts. Life is easier, yet paradoxically more complex. Society has moved even further away from nature making it difficult to achieve a calm disposition with so many unwanted distractions popping-up all day long, incessantly bombarding your peace of mind.

Practice being calm all of the time and record how many hours or days you can remain calm without ever getting stressed, moody, agitated, anxious, bored, upset, or feeling overwhelmed. The longer those periods of calm become, the closer to spiritual detachment you will be. If you can make 3 weeks without one vexed episode you are doing extremely well. We can generate calm ourselves, yet it can be inspired from anything in nature which represents eternity, like a still lake reflecting the clouds in the sky, or large trees overshadowing us with their aging magnificence, hills and mountains rolling out a supportive landscape, or an ocean full of promise. Maybe your parents taught you stressful, impulsive responses to things, or maybe tragedy has triggered stress momentum, or possibly you feel let down by life and society, but more than ever in recent times does the world need you to be calm.

Be casual about things.

Move slowly and deliberately.

Practice light muscular movements.

Wear an insouciant attitude.

Stop when anything feels like it's getting too much.

Be less concerned about the outcome.

Be light-hearted, humorous, fun and see good in everything.

Every move should store up internal energy.

Break the day up with walks, sunlight, cups of tea and little chats.

Think as the air does. Now don't think.

Feel silence and a peace of mind come over you.

Act stupidly sometimes like a silly child.

Live in the present all the time.

Be unconcerned and worry about nothing.

Take your time with everything.

Do a random dance.

Keep your heartbeat low.

Prepare for things to keep your stress hormones reduced.

Exercise within your muscle's limits.

Find your centre of calm, ponder on life and reach a deep relaxation.

Adopt calm mannerisms and speak.

Identify your stress triggers.

Allow other people to be stressed without it effecting you.

Adapt to physiological changes.

See calm as a way of life, rather than just a tool for troubled times.

Cope with sudden changes in circumstance and emergencies.

First there is thought, then movement, followed by consequence.

Stop worrying about everyone else's problems. Just don't.

Find your own pace.

Realize that nothing has a beginning or end. Life is eternal.

Avoid displacement activity.

Intensity is momentum, so break the speed.

Yoda your head and yoga your shoulders.

Smile and laugh as much as you can.

Very few things are actually important.

Happiness is the aim. Calm is the gateway.

A successful voyage into the unknown can only be done safely if quite mad, a spiritual conduit or clock calm. Being calm is the best option available because all of your faculties, potential and energy become metronomic with nature's ancient rhythms. Staying calm in almost all circumstances will help you reach your destiny if you take action like a sprinting cheetah when it's time to. Tension holds you back and passes your future on to another life force. Calm generates its own luck by dividing good and evil into clear options.

Gain a sense of detachment without putting your head in the sand. If you remain calm nothing will scare or phase you. And even if you're not feeling calm it's amazing how far pretend calm goes. Simulate a clichéd calm monk or the idea of your inner place of tranquillity and you shall feel much more capable. We live from the point given and make the best of it with good decisions, plans, stratagems, tactics picked up along the way, embracing good experiences and staying away from what we all know to be evil.

Often doing things slower and calmer makes room for more enjoyment. A constant calm is a uniform trait held by happy people because when we're calm the world just seems to slot into place much better, obvious things make sense and the unknown turns from fear to opportunity. Calm and productive action often silences your critics. If you're feeling truly good from within, nothing would bother you and you'll be able to deal with everything effectively. How emotionally successful we are in life partially depends on the social pace we choose combined with our thyroid gland's inclinations (reducing your salt, sugar and artificial chemicals intake helps a lot too). Yet it is possible to slow the pace of positive underlying thoughts to achieve a timeless calm.

Staying calm is the best way to survive because it keeps your options alive.

Some people are just lucky to be born averagely calm, some adopt a family calm and others are so comatose they lack the drive and manipulation to awaken their perpetually hibernating intuition. Contrastingly, many very smart people are born so super alert to every colour they see, random creative thoughts, comment's people make, etc, that every day is an overload to their burnt-out senses. Ignorance can be bliss because stupidity has the distinct advantage of not knowing how stupid it is. Sometimes happiness is open to those who only reach halfway into their thoughts.

I like the sound of trees
when the wind goes through their leaves.

Through calm comes detachment, until you don the cape of wisdom. Detachment avoids nothing, facing everything with common sense and backbone. Mental detachment feels commanding as it allows you to view your own world, problems and dilemmas from a safe distance as if you were another person looking down from above with a smug grin on your face. Becoming detached makes you the field marshal of your mind. The great benefits of detachment are: increased problem solving; having no anxiety or worry; healing better; a closer connection to your intuition and feelings; it puts things in a healthy perspective; you need less or no friends to be happy; you feel and *are* in control of yourself; it cures addictions; completely stops you moaning about anything; utilises your energy very well; you'll increase your likeability factor; and you won't make bad financial decisions.

The pitter-patter of rain
tickles a stressed brain.

Detachment is free and has no unpleasant side effects unlike its poorer cousin escapism; using alcohol, drugs, sex, violence, pity, social media, entertainment, etc. The only one downside is that mental detachment can initially make you feel superior to others who are clearly wrapped up in their media brainwashed lives; a bit like you're an egotistical conductor of an amateur orchestra. However, prolonged detachment directs you to help desperate people suffering without locking you into their pain. Altruism is like taking a holiday away from your troubles – detaching via proxy.

When I look at a candle flame
I see hope for a brighter future.

Detachment is an important principle of Taoism, Buddhism, Hinduism, Stoicism, the Bahá'í Faith, Yoga, Zen, Jainism, Confucianism, Sufism, Kabbalah, Eastern Christian monasticism, Western Christianity Ignatian spirituality and many other philosophies and religions. This higher spiritual plane is sometimes referred to as non-attachment, a release from desire, without suffering or passion (Apatheia), indifference and detached watchfulness. Calm, kindness and a love of nature are commonly advocated themes to help save humanity from itself. The great Gautama Buddha from ancient India, whose goal of nirvana teaches the extinguishing of the three fires of delusion, greed and hate, said,

"No one saves us but ourselves. No one can and no one may. We ourselves must walk the path."

In the last one hundred years, to avoid the elitism of gold collar professions, humans have had a go at existential phenomenology, postmodernism, being beatniks, yippies, hippies, cults, hedonists, punks and on benefit allowances as lifestyle choices. Many modern, alternative philosophical attempts have been made to reject society's greed based machine and *all* have failed. Meditation is the clear, century's old winning way to achieve mental detachment from your troubles and connect with your feelings without being a slave to them, but it does take time to learn and feel the full benefits. Nevertheless, everyone has got the time to meditate, usually choosing television over practicing being calm, which is not good enough because TV is now Big Brother at full volume.

As soon as you become unafraid of dying you have won no matter the outcome.

Being calm, detached, meditative, holy and enlightened is the healthiest future available for humanity which is currently spiralling out of control towards WWIII. Breaking this wretched chain of predictable human demises starts with you, the individual, as long you always believe you can make a difference to the bigger picture. As Albert Einstein said,

"The world will not be destroyed by those who do evil, but by those who watch them without doing anything."

I've never found my people until the covid plandemic began. Thanks to all of you who seek the truth.

Voller's Books

The Naked Sheep

A Tale of Two Tweeps

The Rainbow Children

Pancake Cottage

Buttercup Socks

Wearing Marshmallows

Apple Rainbow

Made in the USA
Las Vegas, NV
18 October 2021